MARIA PHALIME

Postmortem

The Doctor Who Walked Away

TAFELBERG

Author's note

The names of many of the people mentioned have
been changed to protect their confidentiality.

Where a pseudonym has been used, an asterisk (*)
indicates that this is not a real name.

Tafelberg
An imprint of NB Publishers
a Division of Media 24 Boeke (Pty) Ltd
40 Heerengracht, Cape Town
www.tafelberg.com

Cover design: Michelle Staples
Book design: Nazli Jacobs
Editing: Kelly Norwood-Young
Proofreading: Sean Fraser

Printed and bound by Interpak Books, Pietermaritzburg

 Product group from well-managed forests and other controlled sources.

FSC
www.fsc.org
MIX
Paper from
responsible sources
FSC® C105735

First edition, first impression 2014

ISBN: 978-0-624-05760-4
Epub: 978-0-624-05761-1
Mobi: 978-0-624-06634-7

In loving memory
of my brother, Abbie

Contents

Part I

A Dream

1 | Asive

His name was Asive and he was HIV positive. I met him when I was working at Red Cross War Memorial Children's Hospital in 1998.

It always felt good arriving at Red Cross. It certainly was a change from the stiffness of Groote Schuur Hospital, the tertiary teaching hospital where Dr Christiaan Barnard had performed the first human heart transplant in 1967. Groote Schuur is one of the two academic hospitals in the Western Cape, a world-renowned centre of specialised patient care, teaching and research. The hospital was officially opened in 1938 and since then it has maintained its reputation as a training ground for South Africa's best doctors and nurses. As a medical student at the University of Cape Town, Groote Schuur had become my second home, although I had yet to get used to its traditions and strict hierarchy.

Ward rounds at Groote Schuur were a sight to behold. Throngs of doctors in white coats would wander from ward to ward, stopping at selected patients' beds to discuss diagnoses, agree on treatment options and share information on the latest medical advances and technologies. There was a definite pecking order to these processions, with the specialists leading up front while the junior doctors followed closely, notepads and pens in hand to jot down notes and take instructions. The students would trail behind nervously, desperately hoping to remain inconspicuous in the sea of white. The last thing any of us wanted was to be asked a question.

Red Cross was completely different. For one thing, white coats were seldom worn as they made the children nervous. You were more likely to see doctors wearing brightly coloured, cartoon-character ties, or with small furry toys attached to the ends of their stethoscopes. The mood at Red Cross was different too. Nobody seemed to take themselves too seriously, and there was very little room for observing strict traditions. How could you, when your patients could suddenly begin crying uncontrollably in the middle of a ward round?

I was feeling buoyant when I drove onto the hospital's Rondebosch premises that Monday morning. I had a spring in my step as I walked to the medical ward, and I exchanged cheerful greetings with the staff and smiled as I strode past the colourful murals that adorn the walls.

I was immediately greeted by the sound of a crying baby. And not just the usual *I need a nappy change* kind of crying. This was more like *I'm pissed off and I want the world to know about it!*

"Who's that?" I asked my colleague Toni*, gesturing in the direction of the screaming.

"He's been doing that all weekend," she said, rolling her eyes. Unlike me, Toni had been on call that weekend, and it looked like it had been a rough one. No doubt this particularly vocal pair of lungs had had something to do with it. I walked over to the cot, curious to put a face to the noise. I instinctively reached for the folder at the end of the bed and scanned it for some background information – *boy, aged two, HIV positive, diagnosis: pneumonia.*

---

* An asterisk indicates a pseudonym.

I peered into the cot. He was thrashing his arms and legs about, and screaming his little lungs out. His body was the size of a six-month-old's, its growth retarded by the virus that was slowly eating away at him. He was so absorbed in his crying that he didn't see me standing there, so I stuck my head further into the cot, until my face was just a few centimetres from his.

He suddenly noticed me and stopped crying. Just stopped and stared, and then after about ten seconds his face broke into a broad smile. I smiled back at him; it was love at first sight.

I noticed Toni looking over at us curiously. "What did you do?" she asked.

"I don't know," I answered. I didn't know what I'd done to earn such a beaming smile; maybe I reminded him of someone he loved. He'd been brought into Red Cross by his grandmother. His mother had left shortly after he was born, apparently to Johannesburg, though nobody had heard from her since. She was young, unmarried, and I imagine terrified of the disease she had passed on to her son. We knew nothing of his father.

Asive stayed in the ward for two weeks while his pneumonia was being treated. Every so often I would catch him sitting up, looking at me. And whenever our eyes met, he would smile and giggle joyfully. I felt proud to have been singled out for his attention, and I enjoyed our special connection. At every opportunity I got, I would walk over to his cot for a cuddle and a play.

When he was discharged, I was a little sad to see him go. I had grown attached to him and would miss the little games that had become our own. But more than that I was happy, relieved that he had responded to the antibiotics. At the time all we could do was fight the opportunistic infections caused by HIV; antiretroviral therapy was not yet readily available for use in public hospitals.

Asive came back about four weeks later, just as my time at Red Cross was coming to an end. He had developed meningitis, and he looked like he had aged considerably in the interim. He didn't recognise me, he didn't smile and he didn't cry. He just lay in his cot, passively enduring the treatment that was being piped into his emaciated body. We all knew that Asive had reached the end of the road, and all we could do was keep him as comfortable as possible until the end.

He was still at Red Cross when I moved on to my next posting, and I hoped that when the time came, he would at least be allowed to die at home.

I was a fifth-year medical student when I met Asive, and until then I believed that I could cure people, make them well again. But Asive brought me face to face with a harsh reality that would be reinforced over and over again during my brief medical career – not everyone is going to get better, some people will just die. I've thought about little Asive often over the years and wondered whether this was where it all started, my gradual falling out of love with medicine.

They are everywhere, the Asives. They come in varying shapes and sizes, young and old, but they have one thing in common – they are desperate and dying, the victims of a dysfunctional health system, of poverty and destitution. They come looking to doctors, nurses and other health care professionals to ease their pain and suffering.

But what happens when those charged with their care are no longer able or willing to come to the rescue with whatever limited resources they have at their disposal?

I left medical practice in 2004, just four years after I graduated. This is my story and the stories of other doctors who chose to walk away. Ours is a private anguish filled with the niggling suspicion that we should have been stronger, more committed, more able to handle the daily realities of practising medicine in South Africa. We move on to other professions where the Asives can't find us, and we keep our stories to ourselves. But festering wounds can't heal. The low-grade infection lingers on, feeding off itself and threatening to engulf all around it in its toxicity. It is only when the rot is released and dead tissue is cleared away that new growth can begin.

I do not profess to be a human resources expert and my intention is not to produce scholarly work. This is also not intended as an analysis of the health sector as a whole or as a comprehensive examination of the exodus of doctors from the South African medical profession. At the same time I cannot deny that the stories contained here are a reflection of the broader health care system in the country. Many of the experiences are common to doctors across the board, to a greater or lesser degree. Indirectly, therefore, this book is also a commentary on the health sector in South Africa and the impact it has on its health care professionals.

People often ask why I left and I've never been able to give them a succinct response. There is so much that I leave unsaid as I dismiss their enquiry with a hasty "It just didn't work out". The time has now come for me to answer that question.

2 | Untimely Loss

I was born in the Johannesburg township of Soweto in 1972, the younger of two children. In many ways my childhood was typical for many black children growing up in the townships during that period. My parents had settled in Soweto in 1970, the year my brother, Abbie, was born. They had met two years before, when they were both working at the Natalspruit Hospital on Johannesburg's East Rand.

My father – who had been schooled at the Catholic St Francis College in the Mariannhill area of KwaZulu-Natal and then gone on to study towards a Bachelor of Science degree at Turfloop University, now known as the University of Limpopo – was an apprentice in the hospital's pharmacy. My mother was a student nurse at Natalspruit. She was soft-spoken, pretty and petite – so petite that she was affectionately known as Tiny by her friends and family. When they met she was swept off her feet by the confident and sometimes boisterous person my father was. Her nursing ambitions were thwarted when she fell pregnant with my brother in her final year of study and was forced to return to her parents' home in Soweto.

Like so many black South Africans at that time, where my family lived and worked was intimately linked to the prevailing apartheid laws. My maternal grandparents hailed from the farming town of Bothaville in the Free State. They moved to Johannesburg in the late 1930s in search of work opportunities. My grandmother initially worked as a washer woman before moving on to domestic work in one of Johannesburg's northern suburbs. My grandfather's efforts were somewhat more enterprising – he took advantage of his fair complexion and passed himself off as a coloured "Mr Stevens", earning himself the right to own a small fleet of taxis. The venture didn't last, however, and he worked as a driver for a furniture manufacturer until his retirement in the late 1970s.

They settled in the Western Native Township on the outskirts of Johannesburg but were compelled to uproot their young family of seven children when the apartheid government forcibly relocated them to Rockville location in Soweto. This was the house where I was born shortly before midnight on 14 November. It was my first act of defiance – my mother's wish had been that I make my appearance the following day, her own birthday.

My father was new to Johannesburg. He grew up in the former homeland of Qwaqwa, now part of the Free State province. His family was desperately poor, and when it was noticed that he was academically gifted, a friend of the family facilitated an introduction to a foster family in Natalspruit. The respected clergyman's family took him in and raised him as their own, and facilitated his schooling at Mariannhill.

We were a God-fearing family. At my grandmother's house – where I spent most of my days while my parents worked – prayer was an integral part of our life. Evenings always ended with long prayers and singing, and church on Sundays was non-negotiable.

My mother converted from her Methodist roots to Catholicism when she met my father, though he wasn't much of a churchgoer. He had grown up Catholic and, though he loved the rituals and traditions of the Catholic Church, he saw little reason to observe the practice of attending mass regularly unless necessitated by an occasion such as a funeral or wedding.

As a child I didn't feel particularly impoverished; my basic needs for food, shelter and clothing were always taken care of. It was only as I grew older and became aware of racial inequalities that I was able to appreciate the relative hardships of our daily reality. My grandmother would often refer to herself as *modidi o ithatang* – a proud peasant; we made the most of the little we had.

We didn't have a house of our own until I was in high school. Until then my parents rented a garage in a neighbour's backyard, and my mother did her best to turn the meagre single-roomed space into a home. A cupboard was used to partition the room; on one side was the space where my parents slept, and the other side served as a kitchen, dining room and TV room. Abbie and I would move the kitchen table aside after the evening meal to make our beds on the floor.

Even though I did not experience much material hardship in my childhood, my source of suffering lay elsewhere. Ours was an emotionally unstable home. My father was an alcoholic, and so much of what we did and didn't do was determined by his level of inebriation at any given time. My mother did all she could to manage the mood swings that accompanied his drinking. I grew up surrounded by the constant static of low-grade tension, which would erupt into a full-blown tirade with hardly a moment's notice. I drew comfort from the adoration that my brother, who was two years older than me, heaped upon me. In his eyes I could do no wrong, and having him there made it easier for me to cope with what was going on at home. He was my rock in a family that was often teetering on the verge of collapse. Abbie was more than a brother; he was an ally.

Abbie was as laid back as I was studious. He did okay at school, and he was very popular. It wasn't particularly difficult for Abbie to get in with any crowd. He was one of those people who you instantly warmed to, with his ready smile and easy charm. I, on the other hand, excelled on the academic front. Though our childhood was fairly typical for a working-class black family in apartheid South Africa, unlike many I had two things going for me. My parents were firm believers in the value of education, and they'd saved and made sacrifices in order to send us to Sacred Heart College, a nonracial Catholic private school in the Johannesburg suburb of Observatory. I was also blessed with an enquiring mind and acute intelligence, and I diligently applied myself to my studies with considerable success.

I thrived in the school's multicultural environment, and I immersed myself in its academic, sporting and cultural life. Many of the children at the school came from wealthy families, and I often marvelled at the luxury cars that dropped them off in the morning and the palatial mansions they called home. This was a far cry from the garage that I returned to every afternoon. I sometimes felt like an interloper in this world of wealth and privilege.

Life at home became tricky when Abbie entered his teenage years. He had many run-ins with our father, and I was often caught in the middle. On weekends he always found a party to go to, and he would stumble home at all hours of the morning. When I could, I would let him into the house when he got back, but on occasion I was given strict instructions not to. On those nights I would lie awake, tortured by the thought of him sleeping outside. But in the morning, in quintessential Abbie style, we'd find him sleeping soundly in the car or on the neighbour's lawn, oblivious to the mental anguish his absence had caused.

When I was thirteen, he developed a habit of showing me off. He'd insist that I dress up and make myself look pretty, and then he'd take me for a walk around the neighbourhood, introducing me to all his friends along the way. I say "friends" but it was just about any teenage boy we met – they all seemed to know him. I never asked him why he did it, but it was a clever move. Of course he was proud of me; I could see it in the way he bragged about me to his friends. But he also understood how street law worked in Soweto, and I think that by introducing me to the local young men, he was trying to ensure that they knew who I was so they would not bother me if I wasn't with him. And it worked a lot of the time; I was often greeted with a distant respect, and some even came to my rescue whenever I was harassed by outsiders.

Abbie died when I was only fourteen years old. Bizarrely, he was struck by lightning while walking back from the shops near our home in Diepkloof. In a way I think it's just as well that it was such a freak occurrence; in my mind it was easier to deal with an incident that was out of our control.

I was alone when he died. Our parents had gone away for the weekend and Abbie had just nipped out to buy something at the shops. He'd planned on going to a party later that evening; his white LACOSTE golf shirt and matching sports shoes were laid out in his room, but he never made it back to wear them. A neighbour came to tell me that he'd been struck by lightning on the soccer field between our home and the shops. I didn't get to see his body but I overheard a callous neighbour in the days after his death saying: "*O ne a butswitse* [He was cooked through]."

Abbie's death shook my family to its very core. We were overcome by a mixture of shock, grief, anger and a deep, deep sense of loss for someone who was so easy to love. For me it felt as if the bottom had fallen out of my world; I had lost my rock in an unstable home, the one person who adored me. I felt vulnerable without the protective cloak he had draped around me.

Girls cried hysterically at his funeral; under different circumstances I probably would've found this public display quite funny. And all sorts of people visited our home for some time afterwards to pay their respects. There was even one young man who came to tell us what good friends he'd been with Abbie, and how his incarceration in the local prison had prevented him from attending the funeral.

I sometimes wonder what would have become of Abbie had he lived. At the rate he was going my guess is he'd either be in prison or in rehab. Or maybe he'd be fabulously wealthy, living the life of an international playboy.

Abbie's death was the first in a macabre chain of deaths in my extended family. Within four years, three of my mother's siblings all lost their sons, and another lost her husband. When my father died in April 1989, I started to wonder whether we were cursed. There were some whisperings about witchcraft, but my mother immediately dismissed those suggestions. She'd been brought up in a deeply religious home, and for her this was all God's will. I struggled to understand God's ways.

After Abbie died I retreated inside myself. I buried myself in books; they became my sanctuary away from the drunken dysfunction inside our house. I lost myself in solving mysteries with Nancy Drew or sharing teenage gossip in the corridors of Sweet Valley High. By then my mother was working as an administrator for an adult education organisation and she would bring home some books from the African Writers Series. I revelled in the tales told by Bessie Head, Ngũgĩ wa Thiong'o and Chinua Achebe. So many times I'd be lost in a story only to be snapped back to the present by my father in the throes of a rant. I'd panic, worried that I'd missed something that I should have been paying attention to.

I became hyper vigilant; I was always on the look-out for situations that could trigger an outburst from him. In my child's mind I assumed that my father's outbursts had something to do with my actions or omissions, and I was always second-guessing myself and working to prevent yet another one. I didn't yet understand the complexities of a tortured mind.

As with Abbie, I was alone when I found my father. It was the last day of school before the Easter holidays, and I'd gone to the Wimpy in town with some friends to celebrate. It was nearly five o'clock in the afternoon when I got home, and I crept in quietly, grateful when I thought he was asleep on the couch. It was only some time later, when I saw the odd way that his body was slumped, that I knew he was gone. He'd had an epileptic fit – a consequence of suffering a head injury some years earlier – which caused his airway to be obstructed. I waited with his lifeless body until my mother got back from work. It was only years later that I was able to forgive myself for not being heartbroken over my father's death.

The last of the deaths, a teenage cousin of mine, was in 1990, and by then we'd all had enough. My uncle cried out at the funeral, begging God to stop taking the men in our family. "*Go lekane* [It's enough]!" he shouted, raising his arms up in exasperation. Murmurs of agreement rippled through the church, and thankfully God heard our plea.

I was in my final year of school at this time, and I was desperate to leave Johannesburg and find my own way in the world. The year had been a memorable one, and I remember one day particularly clearly. It was 2 February 1990, and I was in my matric year at Sacred Heart College. For me, the day itself had a particularly tender quality, for it was on that day that my brother had died tragically four years before. As with every second day of February since that fateful Sunday afternoon in 1986, I had woken up acutely aware of its significance, and I was filled with memories of times gone by and musings about what might have been. My mother and I had sat over breakfast talking about Abbie, wondering where he'd be had he lived, and laughing over some of his more outrageous antics. As we sat reminiscing, I had no idea that another event, later that day, would further mark the date prominently in my mind.

There was excitement at school throughout the morning. That evening was our annual prize-giving ceremony and for the matric class, it would also be the occasion when the student body leadership positions would be announced and honours blazers awarded.

Chatter was widespread throughout the morning as we speculated about who would be chosen, and the excitement continued into the lunch break. When we stood at assembly after lunch, however, we were stunned into silence when the school principal broke some startling news. "It was announced in parliament this morning that the liberation movements are to be unbanned and that all political prisoners will be released," he said.

We stood in silence for a few seconds before we turned to each other to confirm what we had just been told. I saw uncertainty on some faces; on the faces on my black classmates, sheer joy. And then we broke into song, singing "Nkosi Sikelel' iAfrika", and for the first time the hymn had a ring of promise. For me, 2 February took on an almost magical quality. It was capped off that evening when I received my honours blazer and was named one of the leaders of the Student Representative Council.

In 1990 my future as a young black South African looked very different to what my parents had known. In the 30 minutes it had taken FW de Klerk to make his historic speech, the prospects that were suddenly available to my classmates and me were blown wide open. We were all on the threshold of a future not previously possible in South Africa. Though we didn't realise it then, the announcement, along with our private school education, opened the way for many of us to occupy leadership positions in business, the arts, academia and public service. For me the future shone brightly with the promise of a successful medical career.

I hoped that I would make a fresh start in Cape Town, away from the claustrophobia and dysfunction of my childhood. If my mother was nervous about me leaving home, she didn't show it. I'd grown up quickly after Abbie's death, had learned to take care of myself. My mother was away often; she spent long hours at the office, at conferences and workshops. I made my own decisions and I was responsible; I'd never given her reason to be concerned. She gave me her blessing and as I packed my suitcases I shut away the pain and loss, resolving to overcome my past and to create a new future for myself. Little did I realise the enormity of the challenge that lay ahead.

3 | The Diligent Student

I graduated from the University of Cape Town (UCT) in 1999, one of the nearly 200 students who made it through the six years of rigorous study. At our valedictory ceremony one of our professors remarked that only 75 per cent of us would still be practising medicine in ten years' time. I was taken aback, baffled that anyone would go through all that training and then not use it. I didn't yet know that there was a big difference between studying medicine and being a doctor.

I loved studying. When I first arrived at UCT in 1991 I enrolled for a Bachelor of Science degree. I'd been accepted to study medicine at Wits University in Johannesburg, but I was fixed on moving to Cape Town and starting over, even if it meant taking the long road to my goal. On the first day of lectures the head of the science faculty gave a speech that I imagine was his standard warning to all new students at the beginning of each year. "Many of you are here because you are hoping this will get you into medicine. I'll say it now – forget it!" he said.

He couldn't have known that his attempt at tempering our expectations was just the kind of challenge I thrived on. I studied hard, my eye constantly on the ultimate prize – a place at the acclaimed UCT Medical School. I was fortunate to be awarded a full bursary by the British Council during my first degree; it helped to ease the financial burden on my mother. I sailed through to my graduation in 1993.

My education wasn't only confined to the lecture halls, though. I partied as much as I studied; on most weekend evenings you'd find me deep in the middle of a dance circle at a residence party or night-club. But I never allowed my social life to derail my mission. Come Monday morning I'd be back in the lecture hall, diligently pursuing my dream.

When I was accepted into medical school after completing my BSc I was elated. At last all the hard work had paid off; I was on my way to becoming a doctor. I threw myself into my studies, starting with the three pre-clinical years that formed the foundation phase of our training. Here we were taught about the body's anatomy and physiology, about the chemical and hormonal processes that allow the various systems to function as a co-ordinated whole, and we gained an understanding of the different ways in which these systems could fail.

I was in my element. My analytical mind was amply stimulated by all the theory, though a part of me yearned for the onset of the clinical years when we would put the theory to practical use. Aspects of what was to come were slowly introduced, though in a highly sanitised form. In our second-year anatomy course, we were assigned cadavers to dissect as part of the practical component of the subject. We worked in small groups, and each week we would come back to our designated cadavers to work on a particular part of their anatomy, dissecting the muscles, nerves, vessels and organs that we had read about in our textbooks. In addition to the cadavers, each group was also given a complete set of skeletal bones to study. We spent hours familiarising ourselves with each one, studying the various grooves and prominences where blood vessels and nerves ran and where muscles, tendons and ligaments attached.

We would chat and laugh among ourselves while working on the various anatomical structures; I imagine an outsider looking in on that scene would think they had stumbled on a bizarre satanic ritual conducted by deranged people in white coats. Such was the case when a fellow student's domestic worker caught a glimpse of a medical student's often-mysterious learning methods. My classmate Philippa* had taken her group's bones home, thinking nothing of having human remains in her living space. Unfortunately when her domestic worker came to clean the house she made the gruesome discovery and jumped to the conclusion that either foul play or witchcraft had taken place. The police were notified and Philippa was at pains to explain to them that the bones were in fact her study aids. It was only when the university authorities verified Philippa's assertions that the police decided to abandon their investigation. The domestic worker was not convinced, however, and she was never heard from again.

At first it felt odd having a dead person on the dissection table in front of me, but that feeling quickly passed. I imagine the brain adapts to these seemingly abnormal experiences, slotting them into compartments so that we are able to attend to the task at hand. This desensitisation was aided by the formaldehyde treatment that the cadavers were given in order to preserve them. It gave the tissues and organs a muddy grey colour and the skin a waxy consistency, and this made it easy to forget they were once infused with life-giving blood. We were never told anything about the cadavers – who they were, where they'd come from, how they'd died – so I guess it was easy to fool myself into thinking that they were never really human.

I never thought to question the wisdom of my being in that environment, given my previous history with death and loss. I was ambitious and determined, and I operated almost entirely from my intellect, disregarding or rationalising away any hint of discomfort that arose. I was so wrapped up in my ideal that even when fate opened the door for me to make an early exit from the medical profession, I failed to heed the warning.

One evening during third year I was required to spend a few hours in the emergency room at Groote Schuur Hospital. I was there as an observer; the exercise was intended to give us a preview of the drama we would face once our clinical training began in fourth year. I stood nervously in the busy casualty unit, quietly observing the buzz of activity around me as patients were wheeled in and doctors rushed from bed to bed, performing life-saving manoeuvres that I didn't yet understand. One doctor noticed me standing there and she paused momentarily from the notes she was making in a patient's folder.

"What year are you in?" she asked.

"Third year," I responded.

"You've still got time. Get out, now! I mean it," she barked before turning back to her work.

At first I thought she was joking so I laughed. But the resignation in her eyes and the desperation in her voice told me she was dead serious. I quickly dismissed what she'd said and forged ahead on my path. There would be countless opportunities that would edge me back to that door.

Fourth year was a turning point in my life as a medical student as it marked the start of the clinical training. From then on the most important learning happened at the bedside, where we learned to connect with the patient, to take a clinical history and to examine the various systems in order to arrive at a diagnosis. We were taught that, just by speaking to patients and examining them thoroughly, we could arrive at a differential diagnosis – a shortlist – of the likely cause of their complaints. Special investigations such as blood tests and X-rays served to exclude certain possibilities and to confirm the definitive diagnosis.

We were based at Groote Schuur Hospital and rotated to various primary- and secondary-level hospitals and clinics in small groups. Each subject was taught over an eight-week clinical block or module, and our rotations depended on the blocks we were assigned. We would all meet back for lectures at Groote Schuur on Friday afternoons, an occasion few of us relished. We were, after all, still young people with active social lives to pursue.

I learned a lot more at the bedside than just the science of medicine. By observing the more senior doctors I got to see that managing patients was much more nuanced than our textbooks suggested. How far to pursue a diagnosis, how aggressively to treat, when to provide supportive treatment instead of aiming for a cure . . . These decisions required a level of clinical judgement that could only come from experience.

Fourth year also introduced us to the complexities of dealing with patients. The doctor-patient relationship requires stepping into the personal space of a patient in a way that you wouldn't ordinarily do with a complete stranger. Intimacy is established from the get-go, unlike in most relationships where it is allowed to develop over time. In this intimate space you are confronted not just with the organs and systems to be treated, but you also encounter the person behind the patient, individuals with their own fears, hopes and crises. This can be a tricky milieu to navigate, as I learned in my primary health care rotation.

The intention of the subject was to introduce us to a reality that was sometimes easy to forget when working in the confines of academic medicine – that patients' social circumstances and psychological make-up contributed to the symptoms that brought them to seek help at a health care facility. A seamstress who spent much of her working day hunched over her sewing machine and worrying about the job cuts sweeping through her industry would require a different approach to the labourer whose back pain had come on suddenly and was associated with a tingling sensation down the back of his leg. This so-called bio-psychosocial approach would enable us to be aware of the patient as a physical, psychological and social being and to understand their challenges better so that we would be more equipped to help them.

We were also encouraged to work in partnership with patients in order to bring about the desired improvements in their health. Traditionally the doctor-patient relationship saw doctors positioned at the superior end of a paternalistic relationship. In this role they doled out instructions, castigated patients for perceived wrongdoing and mumbled incoherent and often poorly understood diagnoses in doctor-speak. This did little to empower patients to take an active role in looking after their own health. We were taught to establish a therapeutic partnership in which patients became active partners in the management of their health.

My group was posted at the Heideveld Community Health Centre, where we saw patients at their first point of contact with the health care system. Most had minor complaints, which was consistent with studies that have shown that only one per cent of patients presenting to health care professionals have ailments serious enough to warrant hospitalisation. As I saw patients, I was conscious of the importance of building a therapeutic relationship and I paid particular attention to the psychosocial factors – such as their home environment and psychological stressors – that could be contributing to their symptoms.

On the third morning there a male patient in his early forties came into the consulting room complaining of intermittent chest pain.

"I've been here before with this, Doctor, but nobody can tell me what's wrong," he said. He looked distressed by this unexplained symptom.

I took a thorough medical history, asking questions about previous illnesses, medication and treatments. In the bio-psychosocial approach it was still important to exclude biological factors related to a patient's symptoms; it would be disastrous to miss a potential heart attack while asking a patient how he felt his social circumstances could be contributing to his pain. As the consultation continued I learned that this man was otherwise well, and he had none of the medical conditions that would predispose him to heart disease like high blood pressure, diabetes or abnormal cholesterol.

Then I began to probe further, delving into the psychosocial factors. "What do you think is causing this pain?" I asked.

"Well, it might have something to do with the stress that I've been under lately," he said. I encouraged him to continue.

"It's my wife, Doctor. She's causing me a lot of stress."

"Tell me more about what's going on between you and your wife. How is she causing you stress?"

"Well, she's always complaining about money. She says there's never enough. What can I do? I'm trying my best," he said.

I nodded and immediately his posture relaxed. He sat back in his chair and smiled for the first time. The relief was evident on his face. "I'm glad someone is finally listening to me," he said.

I was thrilled and proud of myself. I'd made a breakthrough with this man by taking his complaint seriously and probing deeply enough to uncover the real cause of his complaint. Too often he'd been dismissed with the assurance that there was nothing wrong with his heart.

I still needed to examine him, even though the history pointed to family stressors as the primary factor contributing to his symptoms. He continued to smile as he took his shirt off and lay on the examination table.

I was still a novice at examining patients so I started from scratch, beginning first with a general examination before concentrating my focus on his chest and cardiovascular system. I was slow and methodical.

"Do you have a husband?" he asked suddenly.

I was startled; I hesitated for a few seconds but then dismissed the question as mere small talk.

"No," I said and I continued my examination.

"You're a beautiful woman," he said. He looked straight at me. My hands were flat on his naked chest.

I may have been a novice doctor but I was a seasoned woman. I knew a chat-up when I heard one. I said nothing, and continued the rest of the examination in silence. His mouth was curved in a smug grin throughout, and I felt that the therapeutic partnership I had tried so hard to establish had left me very exposed.

Initially I was upset and confused. I didn't know if I'd acted correctly, what recourse I had in that kind of situation. Should I have stopped, refused to continue the examination? Or perhaps I should have reported him to the doctor in charge?

By the time I got back to medical school, however, I had rallied my internal resources enough to view the incident as a learning opportunity. I wrote an essay on it in which I discussed the complexities of the evolving doctor-patient relationship and the challenges that women faced in what was previously a male-dominated profession. I wasn't going to be beaten by this man who couldn't see beyond my gender. In many ways this single-mindedness served me well. I was a fighter, and I used this trait to push my way through.

Though I was defiant the lesson of that incident stuck in my mind. I realised that as educated and accomplished as I was, in some patients' eyes I was still just a woman with a petite frame and a friendly smile. Getting too close to them could land me in trouble.

In fourth year I also learned the value of a healthy sense of humour. As I would later appreciate, sometimes laughter was the saving grace that helped to diffuse the pressure of the environment in which I worked.

I was introduced to the field of obstetrics in the second half of the year. I'd been looking forward to the eight-week block as I would now take on the responsibility of delivering babies.

At the start of the rotation we were each given a blue book in which to record the various procedures that we were required to perform or observe. There were fifteen standard deliveries that we had to manage; in addition we had to observe complex procedures such as forceps deliveries, episiotomies and Caesarean sections.

Unfortunately I began my rotation at Mowbray Maternity Hospital, a secondary-level maternity hospital in the southern suburbs of Cape Town. Women who came to Mowbray were referred there from the clinics with complications such as prolonged labour or gestational hypertension. Many of the deliveries required intervention by an experienced doctor, and there was little opportunity for the students to manage their own deliveries. As a result, by the fourth week I was running behind on my procedures, while I knew that my colleagues at the clinics had already filled their delivery quotas. I was extremely competitive in those days and when my turn came to go to the clinics, I went in like a dog after a bone.

I was posted at the midwife obstetric unit in the Cape Flats township of Mitchells Plain. As the name implies MOUs were obstetric units run almost entirely by midwives. They were primary health care facilities, often physically located on the grounds of a local clinic. Here women with uncomplicated pregnancies gave birth naturally with little medical intervention, but with the added advantage of having trained personnel on hand in case of difficulties. There were usually no problems; women would arrive in labour, give birth, nurse their babies and then go home.

I went into that first day at the MOU determined, but I needn't have worried. Babies were just dropping out, some quite literally. I had a field day in the delivery room. In many ways I wasn't really doing anything. I was reminded that in days gone by women would go off on their own to give birth, that their bodies knew what to do. What modern medicine was doing was improving the chances of survival for both mother and baby.

The midwives were skilful and efficient, and their guidance was invaluable to my learning. I clocked up many deliveries and at some point I was elated when I realised that I'd have more than enough for my blue book.

I'd been working non-stop when a woman arrived in the late afternoon. She had been in labour for a number of hours, but her labour pains weren't the only discomfort troubling her. She had taken a laxative some time before, and the active ingredient was starting to work.

For the uninitiated, it is important to understand that the sensation a woman feels when she is in the final "pushing" stages of labour is similar to the sensation of needing to defecate. We would use this fact to our advantage to coach inexperienced mothers through the labour. "Push like you want to poo-poo," was the mantra, and once they got over the embarrassment of what we were asking them to do, they settled into the process and pushed their babies out.

Sometimes women took laxatives in the early stages of labour to clear their bowels in preparation for pushing. Timing was key, of course, as it was important that the laxative had completed its work before the pushing phase began.

The woman who came into the MOU that afternoon hadn't managed the timing correctly. She was now in full labour and the laxative was just kicking into action. As she started to push she did what her body naturally demanded in order to push her baby out, in the process also evacuating what seemed like the entire contents of her alimentary canal onto the bed in front of us.

The midwife and I stood at the busy end of the bed in silence, heads down, doing what needed to be done. The woman was oblivious to anything except her own pain; I concentrated my focus on the baby orifice while the midwife worked double time to clear away the semi-solid faeces that were emanating from her rear. Sheet after sheet of incontinence dressing was changed as she continued to push.

I was relieved when her bowels were finally empty and we could concentrate our energy on helping her to give birth to her baby. My relief was short lived, though; when the next contraction came it was accompanied by an almighty explosion of wind from her anus.

"Sorry," she chimed.

I glanced up at her face and she looked genuinely embarrassed. I burst out laughing; here this woman was, having just emptied her bowel in front of us without so much as an acknowledgement, and now she was apologising for a fart! Tears streamed down my face as we worked, and I was aware that given the earlier events, laughter was all that had kept me from crying.

4 | An Exemplary Doctor

My transformation from medical student to doctor was so gradual and subtle that I was hardly aware it was happening. I was completely absorbed in what I was learning and observing, internalising it until it became a part of me. We had come in as innocents with big dreams, and gradually over the years we were moulded into the kinds of doctors who would exemplify the high standards and international acclaim of UCT Medical School and Groote Schuur Hospital.

It was only when I was on the receiving end – as a patient – that I was able to appreciate how far I'd come. I had gone to an orthopaedic surgeon for a minor procedure on my foot. On the day of the surgery he casually rested his hand on my leg as he talked me through what he planned to do. I stared at his hand resting there, how at ease he was touching me as if he knew me. I realised that I did that with patients too – touched their shoulder to reassure them, rubbed their backs when they were in the throes of painful contractions in the maternity unit. I had seen how the senior doctors touched patients, how they connected and questioned, how they probed both physically and verbally. I was becoming one of them.

Our training was rigorous. In addition to the whole-class Friday-afternoon lectures, we attended tutorials and ward rounds in small groups, and we were assigned patients to examine and present. Our end-of-block exams had both theoretical and practical components; it was the practical exams we feared the most as they brought us face to face with Groote Schuur's most esteemed clinicians. It was terrifying to stand in front of an examiner and present the clinical findings of the patient you'd seen, and then field questions related to the particular disease. You knew you were doing well when the examiner's questions became increasingly obscure, even gravitating to the fine print of medicine such as the originators of eponymous clinical signs like Dupuytren's contracture or Cushing's triad.

Sometimes this attempt to mould us into world-class doctors was more brutal than it needed to be. Humiliation was an integral part of the way we were taught; it was accepted and indeed expected that at some point during your studies a specialist would grill you in front of your peers – and even patients – in a manner that left you feeling exposed.

As students we were at the bottom of the formidable Groote Schuur hierarchy, with its associated oversized egos, rivalry and one-upmanship. Some fields were more revered than others, certain specialists more specialised than others. A few of the egos were monumental; one lecturer we simply referred to as God for his inflated sense of importance and infallibility.

The students and junior doctors bore the brunt of the venting of egos. I witnessed one particularly memorable incident at Mowbray Maternity Hospital; I was in my fourth year of study and I was working with a newly qualified intern. We had been on call over-night and during the morning ward round the intern, Samuel, gave a report on the patients we'd seen. He was soft spoken and hesitant, and as we moved from patient to patient I sensed the gynaecologist's growing irritation. The tipping point came towards the end of the round as Samuel gave a brief account of the clinical findings.

"On examination the cervix was five centimetres dilated," he said.

The specialist interjected sharply. "If you are going to stick your fingers in a woman's vagina you better say more than the cervix is five centimetres dilated!"

Samuel stood frozen, and then fumbled as the team of doctors and students waited for him to say more. He hadn't documented his findings thoroughly, and he was at a loss to give the specialist what she wanted. For the next five minutes we all stood around the patient as the specialist detailed his every omission and dismissed his clinical assessment as shoddy at best.

The specialist was correct in calling him on his oversight, of course. I think many of our teachers were motivated by a desire to produce doctors of a high calibre, who were meticulous in relation to their work. The manner in which they did it, though, sometimes did more harm than good.

I managed to escape the more brutal attacks; there were petty little humiliations along the way, but none that left any lasting impressions.

As exemplary as our training was, I feel it was inadequate when it came to the hands-on procedures. As a doctor you are often required to perform procedures during the course of your work, from simple tasks like putting up a drip to more invasive procedures like putting an intercostal drain into the chest or a central line into a neck vein.

We were never formally assessed on our ability to perform these procedures. The maxim on the wards was simply: *See one, do one, teach one.* You would shadow a senior doctor, watch them, and then you were deemed fit to perform the procedure yourself. Of course the hope was that the person you were observing knew what they were doing and that by the time your turn came to teach, you would have perfected your technique enough to pass it on to someone else. There were some procedures I never had the chance to learn while at medical school, and only encountered them as a junior doctor in busy wards and casualty units, where the senior doctors seldom had the time to oversee what I was doing.

One of our lecturers, a trauma surgeon, used to say: "Don't waste time on the dead or dying." This, like *see one, do one, teach one*, was one of the dozens of maxims that defined our lives at medical school and the way in which we were trained. We learned to ask intelligent questions and to really listen, even to read between the lines when making our diagnoses. One adage that particularly irked me – not only because it was blatantly sexist but also because it too often proved true – went: *A woman is pregnant and lying until proven otherwise*. Though crude, this was intended to remind us to always bear pregnancy and its associated complications in mind when dealing with female patients. This served me well on many occasions later in my career.

It certainly came in handy when I saw a young woman during my community service in Khayelitsha. She was seventeen years old but her slight build and fresh-faced prettiness made her look a lot younger. She came in alone and was hesitant as she settled into the chair next to my desk.

"Hello, *sisi*," I began. "What can I do for you?"

"I've got pain in my stomach, Doctor," she said.

"How long have you had this pain?" I asked.

"A few weeks," she responded.

Pregnancy alarm bells went off in my head. "When was your last period?" I asked.

"Some months ago, Doctor," she said.

"So you're pregnant, then?"

She shook her head. "No, Doctor."

I paused. There was a level of sincerity in her eyes that told me she genuinely didn't think she could be pregnant.

I tried a different approach. "Are you on any form of birth control?"

"No, Doctor."

"Do you have a boyfriend?"

"No, Doctor."

"Are you sure?"

"Yes, Doctor," she said earnestly.

I suspended that particular line of questioning as it wasn't getting me anywhere and I elected instead to try to uncover other possible causes for her symptoms. I came up with nothing. She had persistent lower-abdominal cramps and she hadn't had a menstrual period in over three months. Pregnancy seemed the most obvious diagnosis but she was so adamant that she couldn't be pregnant.

I asked her to lie down on the examination bed in the room. Sure enough, as soon as I placed my hand on her abdomen I felt a mass arising from her pelvis that strongly suggested a gravid uterus, about fourteen weeks' gestation. The pregnancy was confirmed when I tested her urine.

Sadly, I don't think this young woman was lying when she told me she couldn't be pregnant. I suspect she had very little knowledge of how her body worked; she may even have been impregnated by someone who wasn't her boyfriend, which would explain her strong resistance to the possibility of what I was suggesting.

My training attuned me to the clinical clues that told me what my patients feared to utter. Often I had to read between the lines as some answers lay hidden in the evidence given by symptoms and physical signs. At other times, however, diagnoses were so plainly in view I nearly missed them by searching for more elusive clues. A young man from the Eastern Cape taught me that valuable lesson. He was a patient in the orthopaedics ward at Groote Schuur and was assigned to me during one of our bedside tutorials.

The orthopaedic surgeon instructed me to take a history and examine the patient for later presentation. As I prepared to take a history I was already working through my mind what could have brought a young man to the orthopaedic ward.

I began by asking him what he was doing in hospital, to encourage him to speak openly about his condition. He told me that he had come back from traditional initiation school in the Eastern Cape. He was bright and well spoken, and he'd been briefed not to give the diagnosis away. The sparkle in his eye told me that he enjoyed the momentary wrinkling of my brow as I wondered what on earth his traditional circumcision had to do with his orthopaedic problem.

I tried again. "*Bhuti*, what happened to bring you into hospital?" I asked.

"I went to the bush for circumcision," he said again.

I realised I needed to adjust my approach. I thought that perhaps if I heard him out, gave him some room to tell me about his initiation, he would eventually get to the real reason he was in hospital.

"What happened while you were there?"

"I got very sick," he said.

Initiation schools were notorious – and still are – for their un-hygienic practices and the harm that young men come to when there. Every year there are reports in the newspapers of sepsis and even deaths that occur at the more dubious of these schools. If this patient had fallen ill, then it was most likely a septic circumcision wound. But what did that have to do with his bones and joints?

I continued to probe but I gleaned nothing more than his tale of botched circumcision; apart from that he'd been fit and well, and had suffered no other injuries.

I proceeded to examine him, all the time wondering what I was going to tell the surgeon when the time came to present the case. I ran through what I knew of his story, and tried to match it to the physical findings that were emerging. Most of the large joints of his arms and legs had limited movement, and he had a healing scar on his right shin. A picture was beginning to form in my mind, though it remained frustratingly out of focus.

"What happened here?" I asked, pointing to the scar on his shin.

"There was infection in the bone inside," he said.

In that instant the picture became clear as the pieces of the puzzle slotted into place. His circumcision wound had become infected and the sepsis had entered his bloodstream, where it spread out to his joints and his tibia. When the joints healed the damage had caused them to become fused, which limited their range of motion as I'd found on examination. This young man had suffered a terrible ordeal just as he was embarking on his journey of manhood. Now he was lying virtually immobilised in bed.

As a student I learned a lot from that patient. His assertion right at the beginning of our interaction had held all the clues to what was ailing him; I had been preoccupied with my own ideas of a differential diagnosis, and had been too quick to dismiss what seemed like an irrelevant detail. That young man sensitised me to the importance of listening to my patients' stories, as they held the clues that would help me in treating them.

Sometimes arriving at a diagnosis was a secondary concern, at least from the patient's perspective. But as a student I was chasing a diagnosis, an outcome that I could study and analyse. I learned to cut through the fluff, to work quickly in my quest for answers. But in the process I sometimes missed out on the true value of my interaction with patients. This fact was brought home to me during my gynaecology exam at the end of fifth year.

I was allocated an elderly woman with extensive cancer of the cervix. She was from the Eastern Cape and had come to Cape Town to seek treatment for the condition.

I had less than 30 minutes in which to take a clinical history, examine the patient and polish up my notes for presentation to the two examiners. It was a terrifying prospect and I knew that I had to make the most of the available time.

I got straight to the point. "*Mama*, tell me what the problem is."

Mama wasn't working according to my agenda, and understandably so. She was unwell, had received a terrifying diagnosis. She knew nothing about fifth-year exams; I imagine even if she had known she probably wouldn't care.

"I don't know," she responded absently.

Slowly I managed to extract from her that she'd been bleeding heavily, had experienced increasing pelvic pain over a number of months. She kept trying to tell me about her children; she had many and she struggled to remember when each of them was born. I cut her off each time she wandered to them; I needed a clean and succinct reproductive history, not a drawn-out account of her life as a mother.

When I examined her internally I found a large tumour on her cervix, which had spread to the surrounding structures. I also saw the fear in her eyes. Thinking back I realise that in the old lady's insistence on talking about her children she was trying to tell me about what mattered to her, about the children she'd borne in the womb that was now riddled with disease. All she wanted was to be heard. But I had no time to hear her; what mattered to me was getting to the bottom of her diagnosis.

What I did not realise then was that this would be the trend in the years to come. Over the years I had little time to listen to my patients; to really *hear* them. I worked in very pressured environments and I was forced to strip away the colour in the stories of patients' lives to get to the black and white of science and fact.

It is counterproductive to the therapeutic process that so often in our over-subscribed and under-resourced health care facilities the doctor-patient interaction – which is the very epicentre of treatment and care – is such a rushed affair. The therapeutic partnership is reduced to little more than a hurried transaction in which both partners are left wanting. Patients walk away dissatisfied that their complaint was either medicated or dismissed, and the doctor is left feeling that the need for expediency robbed them of the opportunity to truly make a difference in the patients' lives.

As a trainee doctor I didn't yet appreciate how keenly I would feel cheated later in my career.

But even in the midst of the rigour, humiliation and tough lessons, our training also had moments of magic.

I wasn't anticipating anything but cold wretchedness one morning in July 1998 when I heard my alarm clock going off at six o'clock. It was Sunday morning and I could hear the faint pitter-patter of the winter rain against by bedroom window. This was snuggle-deeper-under-the-duvet weather and I didn't feel up to the seven o'clock ward round that I was due to attend at the neonatal unit.

I'd anticipated this feeling the night before and had prepared by positioning my alarm clock as far away from my bed as possible so that I would be forced to get up to turn it off. I slowly heaved myself out of bed, begrudging myself my foresight yet knowing that it was futile to resist. I showered and changed, and then ate a minimal breakfast of tea and toast, telling myself that as soon as my duties were done I would come straight back to bed where I belonged.

The five-minute drive to the hospital did little to lift my spirits. The rain had intensified and the wind was driving it horizontally against the windscreen of my car. The deserted streets between my flat in Rosebank and the hospital in Observatory were a mere tracing behind the sheets of rain, and as I turned left into Anzio Road I hankered after the warmth I'd left behind. My clothes were drenched in the short run from the parking lot to the entrance of the Old Main Building, and I cursed the hellish start to the day.

As soon as I stepped into the neonatal unit I was mesmerised. The room was toasty warm and dotted around it were a number of incubators, each housing a tiny newborn baby. There was gospel music playing on the radio, and the nurses hummed softly in harmony as they went about their duties. It felt as if I had stepped onto hallowed ground, and all my yearnings of the morning evaporated.

I joined the neonatologist on the ward round, examining each tiny charge in turn as we went along. They looked barely human; more like newborn puppies with their translucent skin still covered in lanugo, the downy hair that is characteristic of premature babies. They lacked the cherubic chubbiness of full-term babies as they had missed out on the plumping up that normally happens during the final weeks of pregnancy. They looked almost too delicate to handle.

For these premature babies, survival was a very real challenge in their young lives, and their growth and development depended on the specialised care they received in the unit. The incubators were there to keep them warm as their lack of body fat made it very difficult for them to maintain their body temperature. In addition the incubators limited their risk of infection and helped to prevent excessive water loss. They were constantly monitored and each passing day represented an improvement in their overall chances of survival.

Though the neonatal unit was a centre of high-tech medicine, Mother Nature still played an important role. As the babies grew stronger they were transferred to the adjoining Kangaroo Mother Care Centre, where they were carried skin to skin on their mothers' chests for most of the day. This skin-to-skin contact was as effective as the incubators in keeping the babies warm; in addition, the opportunity that mom and baby got to bond was an invaluable contributor to the baby's thriving.

By the time I left it was midday, but I could have stayed all day. I had never had such a life-affirming experience in all my medical training.

When I got to sixth year – the final year – I was excited about the prospect of qualifying. I was nervous too. I had seen during my time in the wards that there was so much more that I needed to learn before I was ready to take on the responsibility of patients' wellbeing. I knew the theory, but I didn't feel adequately prepared for the hands-on management of patients, the "doing" of being a doctor.

But these were just hurdles, and I assumed that I would navigate them successfully. I was hard-working and resourceful, and I had already overcome so many challenges in my life. I didn't yet know what direction I wanted my career to take. So many of my colleagues already had their careers mapped out; they knew the quickest route to their chosen specialisation. I was more focused on going into the wards and getting the job done; I figured I would find my fit along the way.

My graduation in December 1999 was a culmination of all those years of diligent effort, the realisation of a dream. I felt proud of what I'd achieved – me, a girl from humble beginnings in Soweto, now a fully fledged doctor. I held my head up high as I walked onto the stage in Jameson Hall to be capped by the vice chancellor of the university.

The real celebration happened a week later back home in Soweto when my mother threw a graduation party. She had provided valuable support throughout my studies, especially during exam time at the end of each year. I always immersed myself so deeply in my work that I struggled to remember what "normal" life felt like. Everything came to a standstill then; I studied and subsisted on coffee and sandwiches. My only connection to the world outside of medicine was through her. We spoke often, at least once a week. Those phone calls were my lifeline and they played a pivotal role in keeping me centred.

Talking to my mom brought me swiftly back down to earth, as I realised that not everyone was as absorbed in my exams as I was. She'd usually fill me in on family gossip or the latest goings-on in Soweto. Though publicly she had always been the model of agreeability with never a bad word to say about anyone, she had a sharp sense of humour that few outside her inner circle ever got to see. She piled it on for me, and at the end of our weekly calls I came away wiping tears from my cheeks and nursing aching belly muscles.

For the graduation party we pitched a marquee on the field opposite our home in Pimville and slaughtered animals to give thanks to the ancestors for helping me to realise this dream. As was the custom at such events, friends and family members who had acquired university degrees were requested to don their academic gowns and sashes, and they took the seats of honour and announced their qualifications for all to admire.

The whole neighbourhood was there. For the first time neighbours who had previously treated me as one of the children in the community now addressed me with a kind of reverence that made me both proud and anxious about the responsibility that my qualification had earned me.

In those final days before I began my internship I revelled in my new-found status and enjoyed the praise that was heaped upon me.

At the back of my mind, though, I knew that the honeymoon would end. I had seen the harried looks on the faces of interns in the wards; I had heard them talk of their long hours and formidable workloads. Inside a tiny part of me dreaded the day when I would be summoned to the ward to attend to a patient in distress.

5 | Diagnosis: "Off Legs"

The emergency room was heaving as we began our morning ward round. It seemed as if every available surface was occupied by patients; the more serious ones were lying on the beds that lined the outer perimeter of the large, warehouse-like space, while the walking wounded were left to find any available bench or chair to sit on. The air in the room was heavy with the stench of stale alcohol and congealed blood.

I was in my third month of my year-long mandatory community service at GF Jooste Hospital in Manenberg, a working-class community on the outskirts of Cape Town, where gangsters ruled the streets. I'd been on call the night before and I felt strangely euphoric as we moved from patient to patient. It was a combination of mind-numbing exhaustion and the elation of having come to the end of my shift. I'd been on my feet all night, and I was counting the minutes before I could complete the handover and go home.

We came to a young woman who had been brought in by her aunt in the early hours of the morning. She looked disoriented and restless, and her eyes darted around anxiously, never making real eye contact with anyone.

"What's the problem, *mama*?" the specialist leading the ward round asked the aunt.

"People are talking to her," the aunt responded, concern etched on her face.

"You mean she's hearing voices?"

The aunt nodded.

"What do they say?"

"They tell her to run away from us. They say we want to kill her," she said, and she looked down into her lap, as if embarrassed by what she'd just revealed.

The doctor turned to the patient, who seemed oblivious to the conversation that was being conducted about her.

"*Sisi*, tell us what the people are saying," she prompted, but the patient responded in a delirious non-language, pointing to imaginary demons in front of her.

One of my colleagues turned to the gathered doctors and said in a loud whisper, "Looks like it's FITH Syndrome."

We nodded in agreement, and I struggled to suppress the giggle that had suddenly sprung to my lips. A quick glance at my colleagues confirmed that they were having a similar struggle, some even putting their hands in front of their mouths to hide their mirth. We all knew, of course, that FITH Syndrome was a fictitious diagnosis, an acronym for Fucked-In-The-Head Syndrome that had done the rounds in hospitals for years. These moments of humour, albeit at the patient's expense, helped to lighten the mood of what was often a depressing experience.

"*Mama*, one of these doctors will come and see your niece later," the specialist informed the aunt, and we moved on.

"Resus!" someone shouted before we'd got to the next patient, and three of my colleagues abandoned the ward round and quickly made their way to the resuscitation cubicle, hot on the heels of the paramedics who were wheeling in a bloody and barely conscious patient. I felt a rush of anxiety as I saw two policemen come running through the door, guns in the air, in pursuit of the wounded man.

We continued with our ward round, all the time aware of the frenetic activity in the resuscitation cubicle just off the main emergency room. The policemen stayed just outside the cubicle, and I wondered whether they were responsible for the man's wounds.

"Why is this man on a bed?" the specialist asked as we came to a man in his late thirties. He was sitting up in bed, quietly observing the activity around him. Apart from a vertical three-centimetre cut on the bridge of his nose, he looked otherwise well.

"I think this says it all," the casualty officer said as she raised the patient's skull X-ray up to the light for us all to see. The man had been stabbed in the face, and the fifteen-centimetre blade had remained lodged in his brain when the handle of the knife had broken off.

We gasped, partly with horror and partly from disbelief that the man was alive and conscious. The specialist quickly turned to the casualty officer who had assessed the patient. "Has Groote Schuur been informed?" she asked.

"Yes, Doc, the neurosurgeons are expecting him. We're just waiting for an ambulance."

I felt drained as we left the man with the blade in his brain. His injury was horrific, but it was by no means the worst I'd seen. I had grown accustomed to seeing patients who had been shot, stabbed, beaten, bitten, hacked . . . There seemed no end to the ways in which people could inflict harm on each other, and it was our job to mend them as best we could.

The daily horrors of my work had quickly thickened my skin. After my graduation I had done my internship in the United Kingdom and then spent a year at home. So when I first arrived at Jooste my skin was still paper thin.

I decided to do my internship in England since my boyfriend – and later husband – was living there at the time and I wanted to join him. I was thrilled to be based in the quaint West Sussex town of Haywards Heath.

This was small-town England at its most charming. Haywards Heath is situated on the main rail link between London and the city of Brighton on the south coast of England. The main street was the centre of the town's activity and was lined on both sides by shops, chain stores, banks and restaurants. There was a traditional English pub at the end of the main street, complete with low wooden beamed ceilings and a large fireplace that kept the interior warm during the long, wet winter months. Here patrons could enjoy hearty portions of pub grub and ale on tap.

Fanning out from the central thoroughfare were the houses and apartment blocks that housed the town's 23 000 inhabitants. The 350-bed Princess Royal Hospital lay at the edge of town and beyond it was the lush Sussex countryside that contributed to both the agricultural economy of the town as well as to its relaxed semi-rural lifestyle.

I'd never heard of Haywards Heath before I left and I was filled with trepidation at the thought of being based in a remote village in a foreign country, totally disconnected from all that I knew back home. When I arrived, however, I realised that I needn't have worried. The

Princess Royal was favoured by South African doctors and nurses, and during the time I was there I was one of three permanent South African doctors, as well as 25 nurses and a dietician from South Africa. I immediately felt at home among my colleagues, though the patients were nothing like I'd ever encountered at home. For one thing, they didn't seem particularly sick. They had lifestyle-related diseases – emphysema, heart disease, diabetes. Occasionally we'd see tropical diseases in patients who'd recently travelled abroad. But the typical patients at the hospital were just old.

It was here where I first encountered the term "off legs", which seemed an accepted diagnosis on the medical wards at the Princess Royal. At first I didn't know what it was – you won't find the term in any medical textbooks. I soon learned that it was an all-encompassing term used to describe a variety of ailments that characterised the general deterioration of body and mind as a result of old age.

Patients were brought in to the hospital by their relatives, often with a mild urinary tract infection that had precipitated the decline. After the acute infection was treated improvement in their overall function was limited, resulting in the old patients being rendered "off legs". These patients would then stay with us for several months as their families felt unable to care for them and we waited for places to become available at the often oversubscribed geriatric-care facilities.

There was one case of HIV during the whole year I was there. She was a young African immigrant who had presented to the casualty unit with acute shortness of breath, fever, cough and night sweats. Examination and investigations had revealed her positive HIV status and the fact that she was suffering from *Pneumocystis* pneumonia, an opportunistic lung infection that is common in immunocompromised patients.

The patient was admitted to the high care unit, and she became something of a curiosity in the hospital. All the medical teams wanted to see her; this was something that many had read about in the textbooks but had never encountered in practice.

There was very little trauma to deal with and what we did see was largely confined to the occasional motor-vehicle accident or to children who had fallen off their bicycles. One night on call was particularly exciting when a young man was brought in with a portion of his skull hanging down the side of his face. He had fallen asleep, drunk, on the train home. When he had woken up he had tried to orientate himself by opening the window to see where he was. Unfortunately this was at the exact time that the train was passing through a station and his head had clipped a signpost as the train sped through. I was part of the resuscitation team that first attended him, and we were all amazed that his brain was untouched when the signpost had cut through his skull. The pictures of him in the newspaper some weeks later attested to the full recovery he had made.

My internship was a breeze by South African standards. I worked in general surgery and internal medicine, and much of my work involved observing and learning from the senior doctors. My role was largely clerical when the registrar and I conducted our daily ward rounds. He wrote up all the medication and performed most of the procedures. We even had trained phlebotomists to take blood samples; all I needed to do was to fill in the appropriate forms.

I spent a lot of time in theatre, assisting with operations. Again my role was fairly minor – suctioning blood, cauterising bleeding vessels and the dreaded task of retracting tissues and organs to facilitate better access to the structures to be operated on. This task involved pulling firmly on a surgical retractor, a metal instrument with its curved end tucked under the tissue to be retracted. The operation – and the accompanying retraction – could last for several hours, and often resulted in a spasm in my arm from the sustained contraction.

I got to know a few of the South African nurses well. We would reminisce about home, and talk about how different life in the English countryside was compared to what we knew back home. Some of them had left husbands and children behind, drawn to the UK's National Health Service by the allure of a favourable exchange rate. They were experienced nurses who had worked in very trying circumstances in South Africa, yet in England the norm for all nursing staff was that they couldn't perform any procedures – even something as straightforward as putting up a drip – unless they had attended a training course to certify their competence in performing that procedure. They would roll their eyes in exasperation. Back home they did the work that was required; they didn't wait for a certificate to qualify them.

The culture of the hospital was formal, with the class differences that were still such a part of English society so plainly evident in the doctors' posh public-school accents and the nurses' more working-class ones. That is, nurses who were not South African or Filipino. The mood among the doctors was convivial; we got on well with each other. And about once a quarter we had a chance to socialise properly when a representative from the pharmaceutical industry would take us out for dinner in an attempt to educate us on their particular brand of pharmaceutical product.

I also worked well with my superiors. At one point I worked for a colourful orthopaedic surgeon who had a penchant for tailored suits and chunky silk ties. He would announce his presence in the ward with a snappy remark or an unabashed flirtation with the sister in charge. He was in his element in theatre, keeping us in stitches throughout the operations with his characteristic humour that sometimes bordered on the inappropriate. During our first encounter in theatre he introduced me to bone cement, the substance used to fuse prosthetic joints to bone in hip and knee replacements. The cement comes in powder form and when mixed with a liquid reagent the resulting compound heats up as it solidifies so that it holds the new joint firmly in place. On that first day he took a piece of the cement and placed it in my hand, then wrapped his hands firmly around mine and said with his eyes glinting mischievously above his surgical mask: "As I say to all the girls, hold it until it's hot and hard!"

I was having fun learning to be a doctor, so I didn't pay attention to the tiny hint of doubt that was setting in. After all, I had finally achieved my goal; why then was my dream not living up to its promise? The discontent crept in like a seemingly innocuous virus that silently enters the body, causing only minor nuisance symptoms like headache and fever. But in the background the virus multiplies furiously, and sets about attacking the organs and crippling the body's defences.

I dismissed the feeling as freshman jitters and a touch of homesickness. I put it out of my mind, but nevertheless seeds were being planted and my eyes were being opened to possibilities I had not even considered. During the summer months, many of the resident doctors took their annual leave, and locum doctors from South Africa and elsewhere in the UK would temporarily take over the care of patients. It was from these part-time doctors that I learned that medicine could be practised a different way.

Back home I'd only ever spoken to my colleagues about the predictable career path of a doctor: you qualify, do your mandatory internship and community service, and then immediately work towards your chosen field of specialisation. You had to choose your postings strategically, impress the right people and get your postgraduate qualifications as quickly as possible. And it was always about specialising; to want to be a general practitioner was seen as lacking ambition.

But here were these locum doctors who were defining their own paths. One surgeon was leaving the profession to ride the last of the dotcom wave. He was doing locum work while buying up domain names and setting up his Internet business. Another, a South African woman, worked only half days at home and came to England twice a year to supplement her income. And others worked to travel; they would work for a few months and then use their earnings to finance travels all over Europe.

I was intrigued and I quizzed these doctors on the specifics of their colourful lives. I wanted to know how they did it, what they hoped to achieve. But this was just the fascination of an observer; it didn't occur to me that I could do the same. I knew that I'd be going back home at the end of the year.

And then one day I caught a glimpse of the possible source of the niggling unease I'd been feeling. I was travelling home in a taxi at four o'clock in the morning after a night on call. This particular taxi driver had picked me up from the hospital many times before, and we chatted amiably as he drove through the deserted streets. I looked at the darkened windows of the houses we passed, and it suddenly struck me how abnormal my life was; normal people were in bed sleeping at four in the morning, not exchanging small talk with tattooed taxi drivers.

I realised then that I had hoped medicine would give me the normal life I never had as a child – stability, predictability, a sense of contentment that I assumed other people had. But the work I was doing and the hours I was keeping were anything but normal.

It was wishful thinking, I knew. How could I hope for a normal life when I had a year of community service waiting for me? I'd seen what junior doctors were exposed to back home; I knew that the troubled state of the health sector and the sheer need that existed would not allow me to lead anything close to a normal life.

As it turned out, a taste of normality was handed to me when I returned to Cape Town at the beginning of 2001. The Health Professions Council, the statutory body for the health professions in South Africa, was reluctant to recognise my UK internship. They threatened to make me repeat the internship in South Africa, but I refused. While the negotiations continued, I took the year off. I enrolled for t'ai chi and belly-dancing classes and threw myself into decorating the house that my boyfriend and I had moved into in Observatory. Towards the end of that year the HPCSA agreed to accredit my UK internship, and I was required to take up a community service post at the start of the following year.

My year of living normally had ended.

6 | Under Siege

I was thrilled when I was offered a post at GF Jooste Hospital in January 2002. The hospital had a phenomenal reputation as the training ground for skilled doctors. At medical school it featured on many of our wish lists for internship and community service. Jooste had the right balance – its location in the heart of the Cape Flats meant that one got to see an enormous amount of pathology and trauma. But it was also close enough to Groote Schuur to offer teaching opportunities and a degree of supervision, which were often absent in the more remote locations.

When I arrived there after my UK internship and year off, I felt ill prepared for what I would encounter. Jooste was notorious in the community for being the place "where people go to die". In fairness to the hospital, people referred there were usually in really bad shape so their likelihood of dying was very high. The situation was made worse by the sheer number of patients who came there; as a referral hospital for the primary health care clinics in the impoverished areas of Manenberg, Khayelitsha, Gugulethu and Mitchells Plain, Jooste had one of the busiest emergency units in the city.

I started out working in the male medical ward for two months, and there I was confronted with overwhelming disease. I had never seen patients so sick, and during the first few weeks I was astounded at how some of my patients seemed to cling on to life by the barest of threads.

And then there was HIV to contend with. This was a challenging period in South Africa's history, a time when our government was questioning whether there was a link between HIV and the disease profile that characterised AIDS. This denialism not only added to the stigma associated with the infection; it also wreaked havoc on the medical wards.

When patients were admitted to the ward we would treat them for their acute infection. Some would get better, depending on how far their immune deficiency had progressed. But for many their disease was too far gone for any acute management to make a difference to their prognosis. Patients died in numbers, and ours was to inform their loved ones and complete the necessary paperwork, a task that held its own set of challenges.

The nurses on the ward would not allow us to include HIV as a predisposing condition when filling in the cause of death on the death certificates, insisting that they were protecting the dignity of the deceased patients. Often I would fight, arguing that merely stating *pneumonia* or *meningitis* was only a partial telling of the truth. What we were effectively doing was under-reporting HIV-related deaths and contributing to the ongoing stigmatisation of the people infected and affected by the disease.

Ultimately I acquiesced, motivated more by my desire for a quiet life than by any shift in my convictions. I learned early on that nurses could be a lifeline for a junior doctor, or the bane of one's existence if they were not treated with due respect. As with most things in life experience trumps knowledge, and a cordial working relationship with the nursing staff went a long way towards ensuring that I was well supported when I needed it most.

For all the death and denial, HIV was a fascinating disease to observe. The infection cripples the body's defences, leaving it open to all manner of infection and malignancies. My naturally inquisitive mind was amply stimulated by the myriad clinical signs that the patients exhibited. The hollow blowing-across-the-mouth-of-a-bottle amphoric breath sounds caused by a TB cavity in the lung; the deep brownish-purple raised skin lesions of Kaposi's sarcoma; the dementia of HIV encephalopathy . . . There was no shortage of opportunities for learning.

But this wasn't an academic exercise; we were dealing with people's lives, and I grew increasingly discouraged by my inability to effect real treatment. It was as if we were just processing patients, shifting them a few steps away from death and hoping they would stay there for as long as possible.

At Jooste, as at most public hospitals, beds were in high demand and part of what we had to do was to move patients out as soon as they were deemed fit enough. The yardstick for determining fitness for discharge was crude at best and was largely determined by the prevailing circumstances. I was taken aback the first time I witnessed it.

We were on a ward round with a specialist who had come in from Groote Schuur, assessing the progress of patients' treatment and making adjustments where necessary. We came to the bed of a young man in his early twenties, an HIV-positive patient with active tuberculosis. He had previously defaulted on his treatment and his condition had deteriorated. He'd been brought into the hospital acutely unwell. We had stabilised him and resumed his TB treatment, and he was making a slow recovery. By now he had been with us for nearly two weeks.

"How are you feeling?" the consultant asked him.

"I'm better, Doctor," he responded softly.

"That's good to hear," the specialist continued, flipping through the patient's folder. He replaced the folder on its hook at the end of the bed and turned his attention back to the patient. "Can you try to stand up for me? Do you think you can manage?"

I was sceptical; I'd never seen this patient out of bed.

"I can try, Doctor," the man said. He valiantly heaved his bony legs over the side of the bed, and he looked as if he was summoning strength he had long forgotten he had. My scepticism abated with each staccato movement he made, slowly raising himself up to stand.

"That's very good," the specialist said and the young man looked pleased with himself.

"Now can you try to take a few steps forward?"

Again the patient steeled himself for a few seconds, and then slowly took his first step away from his bed, his foot staying just a few centimetres off the ground. The specialist nodded his encouragement and the patient took the next step and the next, until he had walked about a metre and a half.

The specialist turned to the nurse who was accompanying us on the ward round. "Is anyone at home with him?"

"Yes, Doctor. He lives with his mother. She comes to visit him here regularly," she responded.

"Let's get him ready for discharge, then," the doctor instructed. He turned back to the patient who by now was looking confused.

"*Bhuti*, you are doing much better now so we are sending you home. Please make sure you take your TB medicine so that you can be well again."

The patient didn't respond but the pride he'd initially displayed disappeared as his face fell. I imagine he was disappointed to realise that the test he thought he'd passed had led to his untimely departure from the ward.

I felt for the patient but I understood what the doctor needed to do. He was being pragmatic; we had done enough for this young man so that his life was no longer in immediate danger. From now on his family would need to be his primary carers as there were many more urgent cases waiting for us to deal with.

I worked one in four nights on call and on a typical night I would assess new patients who had been referred from casualty and monitor any problem cases on the wards. An on-call room was provided for the night but this served more as a space to grab a bite to eat and take some weight off my feet when the opportunity arose rather than a place to sleep. The room was located outside the female medical ward, just off the main corridor that linked the wards with the casualty unit. The constant bustle of activity was not conducive to sleep.

I was fortunate that I had ample support during my time on the ward. I worked with a medical registrar who would supervise the clinical management of patients, and specialist physicians would conduct teaching ward rounds at least once a week. It was comforting to know that help was at hand, though I completely forgot that fact one night when I was faced with a terrifying prospect.

A colleague who worked on the female ward had asked me to keep a watchful eye on one of her patients. The patient was in her mid-twenties and had developed a pericardial effusion as a result of TB.

The heart is surrounded by a two-layered sac and when healthy the two layers are separated by a thin film of fluid with very little space in between. But in certain diseased states this sac can fill with fluid, resulting in a pericardial effusion, which places pressure on the heart contained within. If the effusion continues to grow there will come a point when the pressure generated inside the sac will impede the heart's ability to fill, leading to a life-threatening condition known as cardiac tamponade.

Mariette* briefed me on her patient with the effusion just as she was about to go home. "She's due to go to Groote Schuur in the morning, but just watch her in case."

"In case of what?" I asked, my own heart skipping a beat.

Mariette chuckled. "Don't worry, I'm sure she won't tamponade," she said, and she waved goodbye with a smile.

It was too late to keep from worrying. I knew from textbooks that the treatment for cardiac tamponade involved inserting a needle into the chest cavity and draining the fluid, but I'd never done it before; I'd never even seen the procedure performed.

I was so overcome with terror that it didn't occur to me that I could call one of the surgeons or anaesthetists if the need arose. For the rest of the night I went to see the patient hourly, subjecting her to thorough examination even though her condition remained unchanged. The poor woman grew increasingly annoyed with me and during the evening's screening of the popular television soap opera *Generations* she refused outright to submit to examination.

Mariette howled with laughter the next morning when I reported back on the night's events. I never did resolve with her whether she had played a practical joke on a naïve colleague.

Humour was often the saving grace in the challenging circumstances in which I was working. In reality there wasn't much to laugh about, but we found humour even in the most unlikely situations. One morning at GF Jooste I was on a ward round with the medical registrar when we came to the bed of an elderly man with heart failure. He was slumped back in bed with his mouth wide open and I winced, thinking he was dead.

"Don't worry, he's not dead. See, he's got the O sign," the registrar said as he pulled the curtains around the man's bed.

I stared at him, not knowing what he was talking about. Was this so-called O sign a specialised clinical sign that I'd missed in my books? The registrar laughed at my confusion and gestured towards the patient. "Look at his mouth," he said.

I looked over at the patient and sure enough, his mouth formed the perfect shape of the letter O. I smiled in comprehension.

"Do you know what sign will tell you that he's dead?" the registrar asked.

I shook my head.

"The Q sign," he said, and then he demonstrated it by sticking his tongue out the corner of his mouth.

With hindsight I realise that, though I was able to laugh some challenges off, it didn't diminish the impact they had on me. On the face of it I was coping, but beneath the surface my enthusiasm was waning.

The casualty unit was no laughing matter. I moved there after two months on the wards, and the level of responsibility increased markedly. I joined a team of four doctors and it didn't take long for me to figure out what was expected of me and my colleagues. Sure, we were required to save lives, but the real measure of our success in the unit was our ability to assess and manage patients quickly, refer them elsewhere, and create space for more to come in. This task, however, was not as straightforward as it seemed, because as hard as we were working to offload patients, the people we were referring them to were as reluctant to accept them. Every day we engaged in endless haggling with medics, surgeons, gynaes, psychiatrists and, in moments of desperation, social workers to justify why they needed to take over the care of these patients. No one wanted the additional burden on their already overflowing workloads.

We worked twelve-hour shifts, seven days a week, followed by a three- or four-day break. The four-days-three-nights stretch wasn't too bad, as the bulk of that consisted of relatively normal working hours from eight in the morning to eight in the evening. It was when I worked four nights in a row that I really felt it, because those nights always fell over the dreaded weekend.

Those weekends were particularly horrific. Stabbings, gunshot wounds, car accidents, rape, beatings . . . All manner of violent trauma made its way into the emergency unit, most of it alcohol related. The injuries themselves were gruesome, but what shocked me more were the perpetrators – friends, lovers, neighbours, family. It was very seldom the proverbial hooded stranger in a dark alley. These were people who knew each other, lived together, drank together. And on weekends they hurt each other.

The wheels came off over the Easter long weekend. The trauma was relentless, and by Monday morning there were so many patients in the emergency room that we didn't know who had been seen and who hadn't. When the specialist arrived for the eight o'clock ward round she must have seen the strange way we were behaving. We had long since passed exhaustion and had arrived at that giddy state of surrender, knowing that it was futile to keep trying to catch up. She was an internal medicine specialist who probably hadn't seen surgical and trauma patients in years, but that morning she graciously helped us to assess all the patients and make sense of the prevailing chaos.

It was telling that I sometimes volunteered to go to the Thuthuzela Care Centre based at GF Jooste to assess rape survivors brought there by the police. This particular Thuthuzela Care Centre has been in operation since 2000 and provides comprehensive care for rape survivors away from the chaos of the casualty unit. The women are spared the indignity of having to wait to be attended; their cases are prioritised so as not to further victimise them and to begin the process of restoring their dignity.

The circumstances I was confronted with were tragic but at least the environment at the centre was pleasant. *Thuthuzela* means *comfort* in Xhosa, and in a way being there offered me some comfort and respite from the pressures of casualty. Here I could take my time, take a proper history and truly connect with the patients. After I'd examined them and made careful notes of my clinical findings they would have the opportunity to shower, change into clean clothing and have something to eat before being taken away again by the police. I would have to go back to casualty.

I wore the same pair of running shoes throughout my time at Jooste. Over the months they became increasingly blood stained; I made no attempt to wash them. When I arrived home from work, I would put them in a plastic bag, where they would stay until they were needed again. I planned to burn them ceremonially at the end of my community service. Little did I know at the time that they wouldn't be all I would be extinguishing at the end of that year.

The onslaught at Jooste was not without its casualties. Two of my colleagues contracted TB – a combination of being physically run down and the overwhelming exposure to the infective organisms. I constantly feared sustaining a needle-stick injury. At medical school we had been given a talk by a guest lecturer, a doctor who had contracted HIV after a needle-stick injury with infected blood. I knew that, in theory, the chances of contracting HIV in this manner were low, but with the level of the infection we were seeing I still lived in fear. Thankfully I remained healthy throughout my posting.

The dangers we faced inside the hospital were not limited to the infections we might contract. We were working in a crime-riddled community and the weapons we sometimes found on patients and the profanities they hurled at us were reminders that the aggression and violence that lay just beyond the hospital gates could so easily be brought inside.

I began to feel unsafe, fearing that one day that world would breach the relative security of the hospital's confines. My anxiety sometimes got the better of me, even bordering on paranoia. On the nights when I left the hospital after dark I would deliberately exceed the speed limit as I drove down Duinefontein Road, heading for the N2 highway that would lead me back home to the southern suburbs. I would press my foot down on the accelerator pedal of my little Toyota Tazz, pushing it to the limits of its 1.3-litre engine. When I reached the highway, I wanted the speed cameras to catch me, and I constructed an elaborate plan in my mind about how it would all unfold. I imagined myself getting caught repeatedly until the accumulated traffic fines attracted a court summons. At my court appearance I would refuse to pay, stating that the dangers associated with my work necessitated such reckless driving. I hoped to draw attention to the conditions under which we worked, to be a mouthpiece for embattled doctors across the country so that we no longer needed to fear for our lives.

I never did get caught. Perhaps the speed cameras on the stretch of the N2 between Manenberg and Observatory were only for show. It seems silly now to think that I devoted so much energy to an ultimately futile exercise. But perhaps this bizarre fantasy was what kept me hanging on to my sanity during that challenging time.

Though I didn't become physically sick the environment still took its toll on me. Day after day I fought to pull people back from the brink of death, with more success than not. But the endless tussle with the angel of death gradually sapped much of my initial enthusiasm. I became irritable; I grew impatient and short with patients. Their neediness got to me. I felt that I couldn't provide what they needed, that what they were demanding of me was far more than I was willing to give.

Yet, at the same time, one of the specialists based at Groote Schuur took a keen interest in me and encouraged me to specialise in internal medicine. She offered to be my mentor and to provide the support and guidance I would need. This was a golden opportunity;

internal medicine was a highly sought-after speciality with a long list of candidates eager to make the grade. And I was being offered a helping hand by one of its leading specialists.

I turned it down. I couldn't articulate my reasons at the time, but I was finding it increasingly difficult to shake the heaviness inside me. Not that anyone would have guessed. I had always done a great job of coping, or at least appearing to cope. When there was work to be done, I did it. I wonder now how many of my colleagues were similarly driven to persevere. We didn't talk about what was going on for us. There wasn't time, and the institutional culture didn't allow for it. After all, who wanted to be the weak link in the critical chain that held the unit together?

I felt bad for feeling this way. After all, a good doctor is selfless; she puts the needs of her patients ahead of her own. Before the start of a shift I would promise myself to be nice to my patients, to enjoy my job more. But it only took one patient calling me "nursie" or a drunken gangster yelling *"fokken dokter"* and I'd plunge right back into that dark space, wondering what I was doing surrounding myself with death and disease.

I didn't like the person I was turning into. I felt disconnected from the very people I was meant to be serving. One midweek afternoon I came face to face with the stranger I was becoming.

An elderly woman in respiratory distress was brought in by her granddaughter. She had developed heart failure after years of high blood pressure and diabetes. I was impatient with her, pressing her to answer questions about her medical history that she was too delirious to answer. Later that afternoon her condition deteriorated. We tried everything we could to save her, but to no avail. Her lungs filled up with fluid faster than we could remove it as her heart failed to pump the blood away from the lungs to the organs of the body that needed it. The old woman effectively drowned in her own fluids as her heart finally packed up.

The granddaughter was understandably distraught. And she was angry; she had seen how abrupt I had been with her grandmother. "You're in the wrong profession!" she snapped as I gave her the news.

I didn't argue or protest. I'd been having the same thought for some time.

7 | The Killer Among Us

I was surprised at how out of place I felt the first time I went to Khayelitsha. After all, this was a township like the one I'd grown up in; these were my people. Why did being there feel so alien?

The truth was Khayelitsha was nothing like home. Soweto was an established township, with most of its houses made of bricks and mortar. Though the typical four-roomed "matchbox" houses were tiny, the yards were large enough so there was ample room to play; many homes even had fruit trees growing in the yard. At my grandmother's house in Rockville we had peaches, plums and grapes; after school my cousins and I would gorge ourselves until our tummies hurt. For variety we raided the apricot and fig trees of the neighbouring homes.

I couldn't imagine any of that happening in Khayelitsha. Where did the children play? What games did they devise on the sandy terrain that was so prone to flooding? In many ways the sprawling township was representative of the stark inequalities within South African society. Khayelitsha is situated a mere 35 kilometres from the centre of Cape Town, but in reality the city and the township were worlds apart.

Khayelitsha was established in the early 1980s in response to the high influx of migrant workers coming to Cape Town in search of economic opportunities. The township grew rapidly, but many of its inhabitants failed to realise the dream of a better life in the city. Unemployment, overcrowding, crime and poor sanitation were commonplace; I saw it in the makeshift houses, the informal stalls selling meat and offal on the side of the road, the rows of toilets in the open veld. These were the realities that patients brought in with them when they walked into my consulting room.

I was based at a clinic in the Site B section of Khayelitsha during the second half of my community service. I worked in a team of five doctors, and together we saw hundreds of patients each day.

They would already be waiting when I arrived, their expectant eyes following me as I made my way to my consulting room at the far end of the clinic. I would look at the floor in front of me as I walked, deliberately avoiding making eye contact for fear of being stopped by one of them. I knew that they'd been there since dawn; they had to in order to stand a chance of being seen that day. Occasionally I'd hear them whisper among themselves, "I hope she works quickly," "Is that the doctor? She looks so young," or worse still, "I don't want to be examined by a child."

I saw around 50 patients a day in quick succession. There was no time to delve into their reasons for coming to see me, to employ the bio-psychosocial approach I'd learned so well at medical school. I processed them as quickly as I could, treating their symptoms with whatever medication was available. If on occasion I spent a little longer with a patient the ones waiting on the benches outside my room would make their displeasure known by dispatching the most brazen of them to barge into the room to tell me to hurry up.

The disease profile of the patients reflected the impoverished circumstances in which they lived – a combination of infectious diseases and chronic non-communicable diseases like hypertension and diabetes.

While I've never been one to believe in conspiracy theories, during the six months that I worked in Khayelitsha I have to admit there were times when I wondered whether HIV was not some engineered virus that was being actively targeted at these poor, unsuspecting people. It was everywhere. Patient after patient would come in either showing clinical signs of infection or known to have HIV. Could this thing be in the water supply? Why was I seeing so much of it? Surely it couldn't just be spreading by natural means?

I knew that this was murky territory in which I was allowing my mind to tread, particularly given the prevailing sentiment around the disease at the time. Fortunately I had the privacy of my own mind in which to probe these possibilities and didn't have to contend with the public scrutiny that the then government was subjected to.

It was disturbing and overwhelming. Just as disturbing was the attitude of many of the patients. Whenever I broke the news all I saw was a sense of resignation about their positive status. At times I wondered whether in their eyes HIV was just another item on the long list of woes with which they had to contend.

On one occasion, though, the tables were turned and I was the one grappling with denial.

I didn't know Nomvula* well. She was one of the nursing assistants at the clinic and she would occasionally come into my room to drop off a patient's folder. She was always cordial, a gentle kind of soul. I didn't think anything of it when she walked into my room one morning as I was getting ready to see patients.

"Can I talk to you, Doctor?" she asked.

I looked up from the patient folders I'd been scanning. "Sure, what can I do for you?" I asked casually, thinking she had a piece of admin she wanted to talk to me about. I realised something was up when she sat down and lowered her voice.

"I have this lump on my neck and I don't know what it is."

As soon as she said the words I wished I could stuff them back in her mouth. I didn't want to hear it. In the time that I'd been at Khayelitsha I had developed a sixth sense about HIV. Without even asking her a single question or examining her I knew instantly that she was HIV positive and that the lump in her neck was the swelling of the lymph nodes, which usually accompanies the infection.

I fumbled for a second, not sure how to begin. If she had any suspicions, she didn't show it; she sat looking at me expectantly.

I copped out; I wasn't ready to confront the truth. I asked her general questions about her health, irrelevant questions that had no real link to what I suspected. I was careful with my words; I didn't want her to know what I was thinking.

"Let's do some tests to see what we can find out," I suggested after I'd examined her neck and ascertained that there was no other complaint besides the swollen nodes.

My approach was complete hogwash, of course. In medicine it makes no sense just to "do tests". Special investigations are answers to questions, and their value is directly proportional to the quality of the questions asked. I was deliberately not asking the right questions and I didn't expect to get useful answers.

I took a blood sample and sent it off for a full blood count. I was just buying myself time until I could get up the courage to tell her.

The lab technician must have thought I had really poor clinical acumen because the report accompanying the test results read: *Have you considered HIV?*

I was tempted to write back: *Of course I've considered HIV. I've thought of nothing else! I was hoping against hope for a different result, something rare and exotic to get me off the hook.*

But common things occur commonly. My buying time was over, and when I gave Nomvula the results I had to broach the subject of HIV.

"The test results don't show anything specific," I began tentatively. She frowned, and I wondered if she could sense that there was more.

"The lab suggested another test," I said. I was aware that I was using them as a scapegoat.

"Okay, Doctor."

"I think we need to do an HIV test," I said finally. She frowned again, and I quickly added, "I'm not saying that's what it is, but I think it would be worth investigating."

I went on to ask about her sexual history, learned that she had a boyfriend who spent most of his time working in Johannesburg. She'd never had an HIV test before and apart from a little weight loss she had no other medical complaints. She gave her consent for the test to be done.

The usual protocol at the clinic was to do a finger-prick HIV test on site. It was quick, cheap, and patients were given their results on the spot. But I realised that her being a staff member was an added complication so I suggested that we draw blood to send to the lab. I walked the sample to the trauma unit myself and surreptitiously hid it under a pile that was waiting to be collected.

All the duplicity and denial didn't make any difference to the outcome. The test came back positive as I'd expected. Nomvula was stony faced when I broke the news.

"How do you feel?" I asked, hoping to arouse a reaction from her.

"There's nothing I can do, Doctor. I must accept it."

I was crushed. I wanted to scream at her: *No, dammit, don't accept it. Demand a second opinion. Scream, cry, do something, anything! Just don't accept it, not just yet.* But I said none of this of course. Maybe she was being mature about the news while I was behaving like a petulant child. Or was she displaying the sense of hopelessness I saw in so many of my patients on a daily basis?

I counselled Nomvula about the importance of staying healthy, the need to get support from those close to her, and I suggested she tell her boyfriend. She nodded at all my suggestions, never once asking any questions of her own.

When I left the clinic at the end of the year I sought her out and gave her my cellphone number, telling her to call me if she ever needed any help. I suppose on some level I also wanted to alleviate my own feelings of impotence by helping her in whatever way I could. She never did call.

I couldn't help Nomvula, certainly not in the way that I wanted to. But perhaps just knowing her diagnosis did help her; maybe she was able to take charge of her life in a way that would keep her healthy for as long as possible. Maybe she joined an HIV clinic and was placed on antiretrovirals when they became available.

HIV presented me with dilemmas that rattled me. I didn't know how to deal with it; how to manage the impact of the disease on people's lives. How could I tell them that all would be well when I didn't even believe it myself? In Khayelitsha I saw that HIV was more than just a virus; it was a deadly menace that was threatening the integrity of our communities.

This realisation was brought home vividly when a young man came to see me one day at the clinic. He complained of not feeling quite himself. He had previously been fit and healthy so this listlessness concerned him. After taking a medical history and examining him I referred him for pre-test counselling and a finger-prick HIV test. I asked him to come back and see me when he had his results.

When he sat down next to my desk about an hour later I struggled to read his face. He looked calm, resolved somehow.

"What did the test say, *bhuti*?" I asked.

"Positive," he said.

I wasn't surprised. "I'm sorry to hear that. Are there any questions you want to ask me?"

"No. I'm clear about everything. I know what I must do," he said.

"That's good to hear," I said. "I'm sure the nurses told you that it's important to look after yourself so that you stay healthy."

"That doesn't matter, Doctor. I know what I need to do," he said again, but there was something about the way he spoke that prompted me to probe further.

"What do you mean? What do you need to do?"

He didn't hesitate. "I must get my affairs in order, and then I will kill myself."

I was taken aback. "What? Why?" My heart was pounding.

His tone remained even as he spoke. "I am due to be married at the end of the year. Now I'm told I have HIV. So my wife and I will not be able to have children because they will be born with the disease. Where I come from, Doctor, a married woman without a child is not a woman. The other women in the community will look down on her. I can't do that to my fiancée. So I will kill myself."

He was so clear, so resolved. And to be honest, I got it. The diagnosis he had just received threatened to unravel the fabric of his life, and he was doing what he could to hold it together.

I tried to tell him there was hope, that if he shared his concerns with his fiancée perhaps she would understand. I don't think I got through to him, though. He nodded as I spoke and promised that he would give the matter further consideration, but maybe that was simply his attempt to placate me. I never did see that patient again.

The scale of HIV infection was frightening. What could be done? Independent groups were initiating antiretroviral (ARV) programmes in high-prevalence communities. The international humanitarian organisation, Médicins Sans Frontières (MSF) – Doctors Without Borders – had one of their clinics on the grounds of the Site B clinic, and they were reportedly achieving impressive results with restoring patients' health and promoting high levels of compliance to treatment regimens. I would listen to the success stories told by the MSF doctors who sometimes joined us in our tearoom. It all sounded hopeful, but I wasn't convinced. They were seeing the committed patients, the ones who were owning their HIV status and were taking a proactive approach to better their health.

But back in my room patients would feign ignorance; they were steeped in denial. I adopted the habit of flipping through their folders in search of an unacknowledged HIV diagnosis, and on a number of occasions I found it.

I was also concerned about how the government would be able to roll out a massive ARV programme in the face of the prevailing challenges. Patients were not always guaranteed supply of their medication for chronic conditions like hypertension and diabetes. What hope was there for HIV treatment?

In Khayelitsha the migrant nature of the population further added to the challenge. Many of my patients still had their rural homes in the Eastern Cape where they would go intermittently during the year, sometimes for months at a time. During those periods they were effectively lost to the Western Cape health system. Who knew if they continued to receive their medication there? The state in which some of them returned to Cape Town suggested they didn't. Even in the city the supply chain sometimes broke down and patients would be sent home empty handed with instructions to come back in a few days when the medication would hopefully be available. Though it was not desirable for patients to run out of chronic medication of any kind, interruptions in HIV treatment were potentially disastrous as they could allow the development of drug resistance.

The successful management of the HIV pandemic was fraught with challenges and in my darkest moments I wondered whether this realisation was behind the government's reluctance to embark on such a programme.

Seeing the impact of HIV on a daily basis was often too much to bear. Such was the case when I was on call one weekend evening at Site B. It was a typical Saturday night and as usual my colleague and I were seeing patients in quick succession. Every time a new patient sat on the chair next to my table I'd look up at the clock above my desk to record the date and time for medicolegal reasons. I was sometimes taken aback by the short time interval between seeing one patient and the next, at the speed with which I was processing these broken bodies.

At nine-thirty I stood up before another patient could come in. I walked across to where my colleague Jama* was working and indicated with a sharp jerk of my head that I was taking a break. Some patients grumbled as I walked past the benches on the way to the tearoom, while others openly expressed their displeasure that I was taking a break. I'd been on call at Site B often enough to know that unless I looked after myself and took the meal and rest breaks I needed, I would quickly become of little use to these patients. I ignored the jeers and grumbles, concentrating instead on putting one blood-stained running shoe in front of the other.

When I got back twenty minutes later it looked as if the queue hadn't moved at all, though I knew that Jama was as efficient as I was at processing patients. He took his meal break shortly after I came back and I worked hard to make up the backlog.

At midnight I went to lie down in my consulting room. When Jama and I played tag again at three in the morning the casualty had quietened down considerably and I was left to see the last of the revellers for the night. Unusually there was a young mother in the room, clutching a bundle in her arms. I went to her.

"Have you been seen?" I asked.

"Yes, Doctor. We are going to Red Cross," she said.

When I peered inside the blanket I was startled by what I saw. She was holding an emaciated baby girl in her arms. Jama had attended the baby during my rest break and I checked the notes that he had made. They were brief – a baby who had developed diarrhoea over two days. She was being rehydrated and referred to Red Cross for further management. But there was something else I could see that the notes didn't mention. This was not a child who had suddenly fallen ill; this baby looked like she had never thrived. I asked the most obvious question.

"*Sisi*, has this child ever been tested for HIV?"

She nodded.

"And what was the result?"

"Positive," she said softly.

I added the diagnosis under Jama's notes in the folder. Why hadn't he asked? Did he wonder about the value of asking the question when there was so little that could be done about it?

Suddenly the mother gasped. We both looked down at the baby, who now lay lifeless in her arms. I did not even try to resuscitate her, given the nature of the diagnosis. My heart ached for the mother as she sobbed, hugging her baby to her chest.

About a week later the baby's father came to see me in the clinic. He brought insurance forms for me to fill in. I don't know what prompted me to ask, but something in his manner told me he didn't know the full extent of his baby's diagnosis. When I asked what he thought had resulted in the baby's death he told me his baby had diarrhoea.

"Is that all, *bhuti*?" I probed.

"Yes. Why?"

I hesitated. I wondered whether it was my place to tell him what the mother had told me, but I realised I would need to anyway in order to fill the forms in truthfully.

"The baby had HIV," I said.

He was shocked. Then he shook his head. "No, that's not true," he said.

I realised the tricky situation I was now in. I couldn't take back what I'd said; here I was breaking devastating news at a time when he was already dealing with the death of his only child. I could only assume that the fear and stigma around the disease had kept the mother from telling her partner about their baby's illness. Maybe this sad mess was what Jama had avoided getting embroiled in that night.

The clinic in Site B was relatively well resourced with staff, though we were not immune to the shortages of medication and equipment which were such a feature of the public health system. We did the best with what we had, though sometimes I found it difficult to keep focus on the good we were doing.

I was on call one evening when a young woman came into the emergency room. She was in pain, doubled over and clutching her lower abdomen. I took a brief history and determined that she had pelvic pain and a smelly vaginal discharge, symptoms strongly suggestive of a serious infection of the reproductive tract known as pelvic inflammatory disease.

I could have simply referred her to the gynaecologists at Jooste on the basis of that history alone. But I was thorough; it always annoyed me when a referring doctor simply scribbled a patient's history without taking the trouble to examine the patient and arrive at a diagnosis objectively, so I wasn't about to do the same.

There were no latex gloves that fitted me. This was not unusual; I have slim hands, what many people have told me are pianist's hands. Regular-size gloves were too big, though I usually made do with them as we often ran out of the small sizes.

But this time even the regular gloves had run out. All that was available were the gloves used when inserting a urinary catheter; they were thin and flimsy, not meant for the in-depth examination I was about to perform. I found this out the unpleasant way when my fingers suddenly encountered moisture as I was examining the patient internally.

I was near tears as I removed my fingers from the patient's vagina, struggling to contain my disgust at the smelly discharge now on my fingers.

I was so angry – with the patient for having this disease; with the hospital for not having my size gloves in stock; with the nurses for not moving heaven and earth to find me proper gloves when I so needed them. Most of all I was angry with myself for exposing myself to the muck. Over the six months that I worked in Khayelitsha that anger would mutate and ferment until it became unbearable.

Along with anger, frustration became my constant companion during my time at Site B. I wanted to help, but sometimes I felt that my medical training, with its strong emphasis on the scientific method and the curative approach, was inadequate to give my patients what they really needed. Often they came to me not with medical problems but because I was the last resource they could tap to try to improve their lives.

When the man walked into my consulting room I instinctively straightened up. He reminded me of someone's uncle; he had that uprightness that marked him as a respected member of the community. I had relatives like him; they were the ones in the family who were called upon to officiate at important gatherings and to represent the family in negotiations and disputes.

He looked well with his stocky frame buttoned into a thick trench coat. He took his time settling into the chair next to my desk, and I didn't rush him.

"What can I do for you, *tata*?" I began when he was seated.

"Doctor, I'm not working," he responded. I nodded and waited for him to continue.

"My children are hungry, Doctor," he said.

"I'm sorry to hear that, *tata*," I said, but he didn't seem to register it.

He pressed on with what he wanted. "I'm asking you for a grant, Doctor," he said, and he produced a carefully folded application form from one of his coat pockets.

"A disability grant?" I asked, though I knew that's what he meant. I'd had this conversation dozens of times in the months that I'd been at the clinic. In desperation patients came to ask to be declared disabled so that they could claim a government grant. The application required a doctor's assessment and a declaration that the patient's condition indeed precluded their being able to perform work in the future. The patients who came to me very seldom qualified.

"In what way are you disabled, *tata*?"

He frowned. "I beg your pardon?"

I braced myself. I wanted to let him down gently. "The only way I can sign for a grant is if I find that you are disabled. In what way are you disabled?"

"But I'm not working, Doctor," he said.

"I understand that, *tata*," I said, though the truth was I didn't understand at all. I had a university education, a well-paid job, and I was unmarried and childless. What on earth did I really understand about his life?

I changed tack. I looked through his thin clinic folder. He had no chronic illnesses and had only ever come to the clinic for common minor complaints.

"There is nothing here that says that you qualify for a grant, *tata*."

I could tell he understood what I was saying; his shoulders were starting to sag as resignation crept in. When he spoke again there was pain in his voice for the first time. "The other children tease mine because they don't have the right uniform," he said.

I said nothing, concentrating instead on maintaining my resolve.

He said it in a barely audible whisper. "Please, Doctor."

I looked down in shame.

"I'm sorry, *tata*," I said finally, not daring to look up at him again in case I cracked.

Without saying another word he stood up and left. I was mortified; I had reduced a respectable family man to begging. I knew that I could have helped, that my signature on that piece of paper would have put food on his family's table. And I also knew that had I done that I would have committed fraud.

I made the legally correct decision, I know, but was it the right decision for all concerned? Was it better that his children went hungry and were subjected to ridicule at school? What difference did I make in that man's life? Perhaps it was this unrequited desire to help that later left me wide open to manipulation.

On a number of occasions members of the nursing staff at Site B would come to me requesting I write them a prescription. The story usually went something like this: *My child is asthmatic. She attends the asthma clinic at Red Cross Hospital. She's well at the moment but we've run out of her chronic medication. I don't want to let her miss school just to go to the hospital; would you mind writing a prescription?*

I would oblige. They would pass me a piece of paper on which the child's medication was written and, after making sure that the child was in no need of medical attention, I would write up the requested script. I trusted them; after all, we were colleagues.

One morning one of the other doctors walked into my room as I was handing the prescription to a nurse. He watched the exchange in silence, and then spoke as soon as the nurse had left.

"So you're in on it, are you?" he said.

I frowned. "In on what?"

"You mean you don't know?" He shook his head briefly before proceeding to fill me in on the scam. There was no sick child, or at least not in the way the story was sold to me. The nurses would take the prescriptions to a pharmacist who would in turn submit claims to their medical aid schemes, without dispensing the medication. Instead the nurses would be allowed to take toiletries of an agreed value from the pharmacy while the pharmacist pocketed the medical aid disbursement. It was a win-win arrangement for nurse and pharmacist.

I was livid when I realised that my desire to help had inadvertently drawn me into a criminal triangle. And for a basket of toiletries! What hope was there for poor, destitute people when so-called professionals behaved in this way?

8 | Walking Away

I was nearing the end of my community service and I was no closer to figuring out what I wanted to do with my career. HIV medicine had initially held some appeal but the realities I had been exposed to had soured my enthusiasm.

I didn't want to be around patients and their problems. I felt I couldn't help them. The medication that I was dishing out was doing little to impact their lives. What many of those patients needed was a reason to get up in the morning: jobs, prospects, to be able to feed and clothe their children.

The niggle of doubt that had crept in during my year in the UK was now no longer just a mild, nuisance feeling. It had progressed into full-blown dissatisfaction with the path I'd chosen, like a virus that batters the immune system. Sooner or later, overt illness would result, and if left unchecked, death would be inevitable. But how could I be thinking about leaving the medical profession when there was still so much about it that I loved?

For one, it offered an unprecedented opportunity to touch the lives of other people. When else does one get the chance to deliver babies, save lives, relieve discomfort and bring hope in the face of over-whelming despair? There were few things more gratifying than see-ing a child, who had come into hospital gravely unwell, transformed into a lively bundle keeping the nurses on their toes in the ward; or the patient, who you thought would probably not make it, sitting up in bed chatting.

Patients came to me at their most vulnerable, and they entrusted me with their troubles and their lives. Isn't it often the case that it takes a major diagnosis to strip away the fluff of day-to-day life and to cause us to confront our more fundamental human concerns such as our wellbeing and mortality? My consulting room became a sanctuary where patients shared their fears, challenges and hopes. My privileged position as a doctor allowed me an intimate view into the drama of people's lives. Though often tragic, I also got to witness courage and the strength of the human spirit.

Now I was thinking of leaving. I grappled with the decision. How could I want to give up on a dream? What would others think? What would I do if I left?

These questions swam around in my mind for months, often clouding my thinking. I was conflicted and confused, with no apparent resolution in sight. Every so often, though, I would have moments when, with sobering clarity, I knew what I needed to do.

One Saturday night I was on call at Site B. On my drive to the clinic I had passed groups of youngsters – some just loitering around; others talking and laughing as they walked, presumably on their way to a favoured drinking spot, where they would while away the night. I'd eyed them grudgingly, knowing that some of them would end up in our emergency room at some point during the course of the evening.

That night was no different to any other that I'd worked there. Throughout the night patients filled the benches outside the two cubicles where the doctors sat, shuffling along as they waited for their turn to be seen. They were all injured, most not in any serious way – women who had been beaten by their boyfriends; friends who had fought and then stabbed each other; minor gunshot wounds. I would assess them in the cubicle and then refer them to the nurses in the adjoining room for stitches, dressings and medication.

Some of the injuries were serious. Two men were brought in by another, a stranger who had been speeding his car and had run them over as they stumbled in the street, drunk. He had killed one of them and seriously injured the other. The driver himself had been drinking but I imagine sobriety must have set in quickly when he realised he was probably facing many years in prison.

I worked with another doctor during the night and together we saw scores of patients. By morning the ones who were left in the emergency room were waiting for ambulances to take them to Jooste and Groote Schuur.

I heard the commotion as I was preparing my handover notes for the doctors who would be taking over the day shift.

"I've been left here to die," the man shouted. "What kind of place is this? Why has nobody attended to me?"

"No, *bhuti*, the doctor has already seen you," the nurse responded, but she was quickly shouted down.

"Nobody has seen me!" he bellowed again.

I got up to investigate.

I recognised the patient; I had seen him when he'd arrived at around four o'clock in the morning. He'd been stabbed in the back, the knife making a deep gash in the fleshy muscle just under his right shoulder blade. He had bled profusely from his injury and when he'd come in the priority had been to stem the bleeding and to rehydrate him. His wound was too deep to be stitched up at the clinic; he was due to be transferred to Jooste for assessment by the surgeons.

He was extremely drunk when he came in, which was probably why he didn't remember being seen by a doctor.

I intervened. "*Bhuti*, I attended you when you came in earlier," I began, but he wasn't listening.

"I've been left to die," he spat.

I took his folder from the end of the bed and opened it to my notes. "Look here, *bhuti*, this is my writing. You are waiting for an ambulance to come and fetch you," I said, pointing at the date and time to try to drive the point home.

He was having none of it. He flicked the folder from my hand and clicked his tongue to dismiss me. I turned to the nurse and we exchanged exasperated looks, then I walked away to finish off my notes.

I'd forgotten about that man by the time I drove out the clinic gates. The day staff had taken over and I was going home to shower and sleep.

And then I saw him. He was standing on the pavement outside the clinic, trying to wave down a taxi. He was topless, and the pressure dressing we'd applied over his wound was heavily soaked with blood.

I stopped the car; my instinct was to run to him and persuade him to go back to the clinic. His wound needed attention.

But I stayed in the car, watching from the distance. He was waving his arms frantically at the taxis passing by, the aggression I'd witnessed earlier plainly evident in his gestures. I watched in silence as a taxi finally stopped and he got in. When it drove off I engaged my gears and resumed my journey home.

For some time I had been asking for answers about the direction that my professional career needed to take, and right there was a sign. After all, what kind of doctor drives away from a patient in need?

My career ended with a whimper rather than a bang. After my community service I applied for and was offered a medical officer position in an HIV treatment centre that would later became part of the Desmond Tutu HIV Foundation. The opportunity would have meant working with some of the most prominent leaders in HIV medicine in South Africa. They were engaged in pioneering work setting up and running antiretroviral therapy programmes in impoverished communities.

The call came in as I was walking to Newlands Cricket Ground with my fiancé and some friends to watch a match in the 2003 Cricket World Cup. We had just been through the turnstiles and were making our way to the grass embankment where we would settle in our deck chairs for most of the day. The conversation was brief; I was asked if I would be taking up the post and I said no. Like being asked if I wanted vanilla or chocolate and choosing vanilla because that's what I felt like that day. There was no fanfare to mark the life-changing decision I made.

I wasn't really thinking. At no point during that brief conversation did I wonder what I would do, what the future held for me. I had a vague sense that I was being foolish, but as I looked out onto the cricket ground and glimpsed the excitement of people rushing to book a spot on the grass and to stock up on refreshments before the start of the match, I didn't care. The thought of sitting in a clinic full of sick people didn't appeal to me at all.

Until then I hadn't fully made the decision to leave my profession, though in my heart I knew that I ultimately would. I was sitting on the fence, and when my hand was finally forced by that call, I followed my gut. For someone who was so used to weighing up pros and cons and analysing her every move, this decision was in sharp contrast to how I was usually inclined to operate. Now, on an impulse, I had altered the trajectory of my professional life. I didn't say anything to my companions when the call ended and I slotted back into the pre-match preparations.

With a career in HIV medicine down the drain I needed to create something new. What, though? I didn't know anything else. I had no other skills. For so many years I'd only ever thought of myself as a doctor and I'd worked hard to get there. Medicine had been a dream I had cherished for so long that I hadn't left room for other possibilities.

I cobbled together the exit strategy, which I perhaps should have formulated prior to that fateful call during the Cricket World Cup. First I had to live, so I registered with a locum agency and sent word out to friends to let them know I was looking for part-time work. There was no shortage of opportunities. I filled in at GP practices when the proprietors went on leave and I worked in community health clinics all over the peninsula.

I worked like an automaton, just getting through the patients. I had no vested interest and my heart wasn't in it. If anything locums served to reinforce my intention to leave the medical profession altogether.

The GP locums were the worst. When I arrived at my first posting at a practice in the township of Nyanga the doctor was there to brief me on how he liked to run his surgery.

"Always ask patients whether they are paying cash or on medical aid," he began.

"Why?" I'd only ever worked in the public sector and had never dealt with the admin side of patient consultations. I didn't understand why I needed to concern myself with that now.

He led me to the small dispensary adjacent to the consulting room and pointed to the shelf on the right. "These are for the medical aid patients. The cash patients get those medicines over there," he said, pointing to the shelf on the opposite side of the room.

I was instantly put off. What happened to prescribing and dispensing medication based on clinical indicators? My displeasure turned to anger later when I was looking through the meagre medication allocated to cash patients and discovered that many had passed their expiry date.

It became obvious at the GP practices that patients came primarily to be booked off work. And what's more, that they were used to getting their own way. They'd try to sell me some half-baked story about how they needed a week off work in order to recover from a simple cold or another minor ailment. I spent a lot of time explaining that, though sick leave was part of their entitlement in terms of their basic conditions of employment, they were only eligible to take it when they were actually sick.

I had honed my sick-note speech at Site B. When I first arrived there I was naïve, thinking that an extra day or two off work was actually helping my patients. At other times I felt sorry for them.

A young woman came to see me in my first month at Site B. She made no bones about why she had come. "I need three days off, Doctor," she said when I asked.

"Are you sick?"

"No."

"So why do you need three days off?"

"I must go to a funeral in the Eastern Cape. My aunt has died."

"Can you not take family responsibility leave?" I asked, but she shook her head.

"I've already used it up. Four of my relatives have died recently and each time I took leave to go and bury them in the Eastern Cape. But after the last time my employer told me that she was fed up with me taking so much time off. She said I couldn't take any more or else she'd fire me."

I kept quiet.

"I have to go to the funeral, Doctor. She's my mother's sister," she said finally.

I understood her dilemma. If she took time off work again without a credible medical reason she would no doubt lose her job. But I also understood the cultural imperative that required her to attend her aunt's funeral or risk being ostracised by her family. I gave her the three days off.

But it didn't sit right with me. Once I'd opened that door I felt like I no longer had a leg to stand on when refusing to give time off to others. I devised a plan. I had to make them understand that this type of leave was distinct from annual leave, that it didn't constitute "free days" that could be used as and when they felt like it. The patients would look at me blankly when I explained all of this to them, so I made up a rather far-fetched scenario instead. "What if I gave you the time off and you went and robbed a bank? When arrested you could say that you couldn't have done it because you were sick; you'd have a doctor's certificate to prove it."

For some reason the patients understood and readily accepted this bizarre explanation and it became my standard response when I was asked for a certificate that wasn't medically warranted. In reality, though, I didn't have many of these battles at Site B as many of my patients simply didn't have jobs to skive off from. It was only when I started working at GP practices that this became a daily struggle. I often got the impression that, by paying a fee to be seen, the patients felt entitled to demand as much sick leave as they wished.

One man didn't even bother selling me a story. I was working at a practice in Langa Township, about halfway between the Cape Town city centre and the Cape Town International Airport. Langa is an old township, much like Soweto. Here, for the first time, I could relate to the patients and I felt far more at home than I had in Khayelitsha. But that didn't mean I enjoyed myself any more.

When the man came in he simply asked for a week off work. When I refused, citing his obvious absence of ill health as my reason, he protested. "The other doctor always gives it to me."

I stood my ground. "I'm not him," I said.

He stared at me, but I wasn't budging. He left in a huff.

Later when I left the consulting room to get medication for another patient I saw the man again. He had phoned the other partner in the practice to come and give him his sick certificate. The doctor acknowledged me with a brief nod and then continued to give the patient what he wanted.

The days became predictable – the patients would come in with a complaint, sometimes real and at other times fabricated. I would treat them, taking into account the particular rules and protocols of the surgery. A battle over sick leave would sometimes ensue, the patients would leave and I would get ready to do it all over again. It was mind-numbing, a waste of my training and by now considerable skill.

Thankfully there were times when the monotony was broken, sometimes in unexpected ways. I was filling in for a GP in Grassy Park when a woman came in with her child, who was probably around two years old. The little girl was at the stage in her young life when she was fond of trying out new words. As I took a medical history from the mother to determine why she'd come to see me I heard a sound coming from where the child was standing, but it seemed so unlikely that she could have said it that I assumed I'd heard incorrectly.

"*Poes.*"

The mother didn't react so I made nothing of it and carried on with the consultation. But sure enough, less than a minute later it came again, and this time there was no mistaking that the child had said it.

"*Poes,*" she said.

The mother pulled the child close to her. "*Bly stil,*" she scolded.

The little girl did as she was told for a few seconds but I imagine the thrill of commanding the attention of two adults in this way was far too irresistible.

"*Poes,*" she said again.

By now her mother looked thoroughly embarrassed and in some misguided attempt to shut the child up she slapped her lightly on the mouth. The child was not deterred.

"*Poes.*"

Slap.

"*Poes.*"

Slap.

"*Poes.*"

Eventually I had to intervene, trying hard to mask my amusement behind an authoritative doctor voice. "She's just repeating what she hears at home. Please try to be more careful with your language in future."

The memory of that foul-mouthed little girl lingered throughout the rest of my time at that surgery. She changed the complexion of my brief stint there and I would often chuckle to myself as I played that unexpected scene back in my mind.

I had never considered establishing my own practice and during the time that I spent as a locum I developed a distinct distaste for private-sector medicine. I was conscious of the fact that this was a tiny fragment of private health care in general, but it was enough to put me off completely.

I realised also that, after the high drama of Jooste and Site B, the coughs and colds were an anticlimax. This fact was brought home to me one day as I was seeing and treating patients at a practice in the predominantly coloured township of Bishop Lavis. I was close to tears with boredom when a woman walked in pushing her elderly mother in a wheelchair.

"What can I do for you?" I asked.

"My mother isn't well, Doctor. She's getting very weak and I'm worried," the daughter said.

I glanced at the mother who indeed looked weak and pale.

"How long has she been like that?" I asked.

"For about a week now, Doctor," she said.

I wasn't convinced. The old lady looked like she had been ill for a while, the kind of patient who had a number of chronic illnesses ticking away at the same time. From the look of her it was unlikely that she was fit and healthy before the current episode of worsening ill health.

"Is your mother taking any medication?" I asked.

"Yes, Doctor. She takes half a Disprin for her heart and medicine for high blood," she said.

I probed further.

"Has she started taking anything new lately? Has she had any kind of infection that could have triggered this state?"

She paused for a few seconds. "Well, she was complaining of pain in her joints, so we bought her Brufen from the chemist."

My ears started prickling. Ibuprofen is a strong anti-inflammatory agent; it can wreak havoc on the stomach of an old lady who is already on aspirin to thin her blood. My heart rate quickened as I realised that I may have a real medical case in front of me.

"Tell me exactly what you've noticed lately," I prompted.

"Doctor, she started complaining of pain in her joints. She has arthritis but it's usually not too bad. So when she said her joints were sore I went and bought Brufen at the chemist. It seemed to help so she carried on taking it. But she's been getting weak, and she's not herself. She's now even too weak to go to the toilet by herself and

I've had to help her." She paused. "I saw that her poo is very dark," she added.

I felt the adrenalin surge instantly. From the history it was likely that the old lady was bleeding from her stomach, a consequence of the powerful anti-inflammatory drug and the aspirin. I got to work, stepping into the emergency-room drill that I had practised so many times during my community service. I examined the patient, found that she indeed showed signs of an upper gastrointestinal tract bleed. I then put up a slow drip and arranged for an ambulance to be called.

As I prepared the referral notes the fact that I was so excited wasn't lost on me. Had I become desensitised to such a degree that only extreme suffering – in this case, in the form of life-threatening internal bleeding – could arouse my interest? I resolved to leave medicine as quickly as possible and I set in motion the necessary actions.

In May 2003 I enrolled on the University of South Africa's Management Development Programme in preparation for a life outside the profession. It was a one-year course, taken via correspondence, with two week-long on-site sessions during the year. The rest of the time I worked through the material on my own and joined a study group that met once a week.

I was still doing locums so all that I was learning about the business world was purely theoretical. Unlike the rest of my study group who worked in industry, I had little prior concept of the subjects that formed the core of the course – strategy, marketing, accounting, economics, operations and human resource management. But it didn't matter. I was paving my way out, and I soaked it all up and relished the real-life case studies that my colleagues offered.

I also began a programme of finding out what other people did for a living. I asked a friend of mine who worked in public relations to arrange a meeting for me with her colleagues. During the 40 minutes I was with them, I interrogated them on what their work entailed, the highs and lows and the long-term prospects. They accommodated my questions graciously. They in turn referred me to others and over a number of weeks I met with people in marketing, asset management, people development, advertising and events. I also began scouting the newspapers for opportunities and putting the word out with friends. There was no field that immediately appealed to me, but that wasn't really the point. It was enough that I knew where I no longer wanted to be.

I didn't entertain going into the industries allied to medicine like pharmaceuticals or medical aid schemes. These seemed like logical options, but for me they represented a sideways shift. I wanted out altogether.

Early in 2004 I saw an advert in the newspaper – a government-funded organisation was looking for graduates who wanted to make a difference, liked to travel and were willing to learn. It sounded like a fitting description of where I was and I jumped at the opportunity, arranging a meeting with Ismail Dockrat, the then CEO of the Western Cape's trade and investment promotion agency, Wesgro.

When the end came it was swift, a surgical clearing. On Friday 30 April 2004 I was treating coughs and colds at a GP practice in Mitchells Plain. On Monday 3 May I officially left the medical profession and began my post as portfolio manager in investment promotion at Wesgro. No more needy patients, no more HIV, no more blood and guts. Just like that.

I felt both elated and terrified that I'd actually gone through with it. I'd done the unthinkable – I'd stopped being a doctor. And more than that, I'd given up on a long-held dream.

To say that the learning curve at Wesgro was steep would be an understatement. Everything in this new environment was alien to me: the content – economics, trade and investment, destination marketing; working with government officials; interfacing with business leaders and foreign investors. I struggled just to get my head space right, to learn to use parts of my brain that had so far not been exercised. In the early days I couldn't even fit into the organisational culture; it made little sense to me why a report deadline or briefing notes for a provincial minister were treated like matters of life and death. I knew life and death, and destination marketing was far from it.

On the outside I was doing well. Friends would often remark on the courage I'd displayed by choosing to carve my own path. I didn't feel courageous, though. I felt more like a fraud, pretending to have made a powerful decision when in effect I'd forced myself to start again in a foreign field I knew little about. I had a chance at greatness and I blew it. I had spent nine years at university, obtained two degrees and qualified in one of the most highly regarded professions. I'd even been offered the opportunity to become a specialist physician, to walk in the hallowed corridors of academia as one of the anointed ones.

For the first time I was able to empathise with my father. It must have been such a big deal for him, growing up in a poor family, to have completed school and then gone on to study at university. But he hadn't made the most of the opportunities that life had presented to him.

I wrestled with similar demons, and yet in my heart I knew I'd made the right decision. Why was it that I had so much certainty and yet all the evidence suggested I was still lost?

My mother didn't question my decision. For the first time I wished she had. Perhaps if I'd been forced to carefully consider what I was doing I would have thought more critically and planned my future more intelligently. Instead I was left to drift, searching for the fulfilment that had thus far eluded me.

I think it must have been quite a relief for my husband, who I had married in the final months of my medical career at the end of 2003. He had witnessed so much of my anguish and had done his best to buffer the pain with love and support. At least now I had a chance to start again and be happy in my new career.

It was true that I'd found some measure of happiness, though deep down I still harboured pain for the dream I had given up. I didn't like it when people asked me why I left medical practice; I would fob them off quickly and then change the subject. Medicine became my private shame, the thing that I didn't talk about. When I took my daughter to the doctor I would feign ignorance at the medical jargon. Sometimes though, especially when I didn't agree with the doctor's approach, I couldn't help but make my thoughts known, even if it meant outing myself as one of them.

I stayed at Wesgro until 2007 and then left to be a work-from-home mother. I started a consultancy and worked with government agencies, municipalities and overseas investors, doing much the same work I'd done at Wesgro in research and business facilitation. The venture chugged along, with some months better than others, though it was never a resounding success. There were some months early on when I wouldn't earn a cent.

In 2009 I was offered the opportunity of a lifetime. I joined the 2010 Co-ordinating Unit in the Western Cape government's Department of the Premier. We were responsible for the co-ordination of provincial initiatives related to South Africa's hosting of the 2010 FIFA World Cup. It was an exciting time, and I loved every minute of that momentous period in our country's history. But when the mega event ended and we submitted our final reports at the end of August 2010, I found myself in that same place again, staring at an old wound that was still to heal.

People continued to ask the uncomfortable questions, and my own internal dialogue was getting louder. As much as I had loved working on the World Cup, and as much as I didn't regret leaving medicine, unfinished business was beckoning. I had tried to keep the door shut, and for many years it had remained so. But increasingly it was taking too much effort to keep the memories and the questions I had avoided since 2004 at bay.

Why did I leave the medical profession? Did I give up too soon, bail out at the first sign of a challenge? Don't all jobs start as mine had, with the most unpleasant tasks delegated to the junior staff and the privilege of doing the more gratifying work only earned over time?

I also know that there was so much more to it than the misery – there were the babies I held in my arms; the gratitude that patients expressed when my actions brought them relief from their pain. At some point I seriously considered specialising in HIV medicine because I wanted to change the course of this devastating disease. What happened to my hopes and aspirations? Was I foolish in wanting more when I had already achieved so much?

It was time to find answers to all these questions.

Part II

Postmortem

9 | A Morbid Enquiry

When a person dies unexpectedly, a postmortem is conducted in order to uncover the cause of death. The corpse is dissected, every organ is examined for signs of disease, and specimens of blood and body tissues are sent to the lab for in-depth analysis. All the evidence is painstakingly put together until a definitive cause of death is found. "Ruptured aneurysm", "cardiac failure", "septicaemia" the autopsy report will read. Armed with a diagnosis, family and friends are able to name the intruder that has taken their loved one, and they can start to make sense of the loss.

My story bears all the hallmarks of an unnatural death. I had gone into medical school with a desire to make a difference, to cure disease and to improve health care in South Africa. But after just four years of practice I left, shutting the door firmly behind me. What drove me to make such a drastic change? Was there anything I could have salvaged from those years of diligent study?

As I began the enquiry into my decision to leave the medical profession, revisiting the events and experiences that contributed to the decision, I was struck by how similar what I was attempting to do was to a postmortem examination. I had attended a number of autopsies as a student and I remembered how the pathologists dissected the various organs and sifted through the accumulated evidence to arrive at a cause of death. But the memories were frustratingly distant and I wanted to remind myself of the procedure. On a whim I submitted a request to Salt River Mortuary to observe a real post-mortem. Perhaps a part of me also hoped that the jolt would aid my own process.

When the day of the autopsy arrived in January 2013 I wondered whether I'd been hasty and foolish. Did I really want to be back in the blood and guts of it all? My curiosity got the better of me, though, and as I got ready I reminded myself to wear comfortable clothes and to have a light breakfast. Who knew what awaited me there?

Salt River Mortuary is one of the busiest pathology laboratories in the country and is the operational base of the University of Cape Town's department of forensic medicine and toxicology. The facility is located in the former industrial hub of Salt River, just five minutes from Groote Schuur Hospital. In recent years Salt River has become shabbier than it used to be, as many of the clothing and textile factories that had been at the core of its manufacturing capacity have since closed, making way for the drug trade and its associated ills.

The mortuary serves the greater Cape metropolitan area, and as a forensic pathology laboratory its primary function is to uncover the causes of sudden or unnatural injuries and death. In addition specialists at the mortuary are involved in research, policy advocacy, health promotion, as well as the teaching and mentoring of medical and law students.

I was aware of the pioneering work that had been done there, in particular by its chief specialist Professor Lorna Martin, in the medicolegal investigation of sexual violence against women and children. This work has won international acclaim and has helped to give

South Africa the rather unfortunate distinction as one of the world's leading authorities on the pathology of rape. This was what I feared witnessing when I arrived at the mortuary.

I had been to the mortuary on a number of occasions as a medical student. We were required to go there for the practical component of our forensic medicine rotation in fifth year, and our first visit served as a dramatic introduction to the subject. We arrived at a busy mortuary that was ill prepared to host a group of wide-eyed students. The teaching staff was away, and all the technicians seemed to want to do was get on with their work. They left us to wander around the place, perhaps thinking that what we would see would provide us with ample opportunity for learning.

In one corner was a family of four, victims of a shack fire in an informal settlement on the Cape Flats. Their charred bodies had assumed a contracted posture – the so-called pugilistic attitude for its resemblance to the stance that a pugilist (boxer) takes when defending himself against an opponent. The heat caused the muscles to shorten and stiffen, resulting in flexion at the knees, hips, elbows and neck and the contraction of the hand into a fist.

Next to them lay a couple locked in their final embrace, their bodies bloated and crawling with maggots. They had been having an affair, and the woman's husband had hunted them down to their rendezvous point and shot them while they were still in the throes of passion. Their bodies, which had started to decompose, had been lying in the veld for a number of days before they were discovered. I had to work hard to keep the contents of my stomach down as the putrid stench filled the room and a technician attempted to flush the maggots down the drainable floor with a hose.

These memories came flooding back as I drove to the mortuary, and I prayed that the morning's case would be relatively normal. I especially didn't want to encounter a victim of sexual assault, so I was relieved when I arrived to find a more conventional case – a gangster, someone whose long-term prospects were probably only ever limited to death or imprisonment.

I joined a group of fifth-year students around the corpse, all of us clad in surgical greens and rubber boots, with face masks draped loosely around our necks. The room had been scrubbed clean, and I was impressed that the chaos I'd previously encountered here was nowhere in evidence. There was a single steel table in the middle of the room where the corpse was lying, conveniently positioned above a floor drain. A variety of instruments were on the work surface against the left-hand wall, some of which I recognised from my student days. The faint smell of disinfectant hung in the air, and mingled with it was the unmistakable odour of a life snuffed out.

There were ten of us around the body – eight students, the pathologist and me. A technician stood to the side, looking on. The students seemed unfazed by what they were about to witness, and I was reminded that this was part of the training, a learned detachment that was in many ways a necessary coping mechanism for the profession.

I turned my attention to the pathologist as he gave a brief history of the case. The subject was a twenty-year-old male from Grassy Park, a casualty of the gang violence that had gripped the Cape Flats in recent years. He was brought in to Groote Schuur two days before with a single gunshot wound to the abdomen. On arrival he was unresponsive, with a thready pulse, and showing signs of massive blood loss. Attempts to resuscitate him were unsuccessful, and he now lay on the cold steel examination table in front of us, ready for an in-depth postmortem examination.

The pathologist began with an external examination, and I was instantly transported back to my student days, listening to every detail and making notes as necessary. We found nothing remarkable on general examination – he was a young black man with a lean build and no external features that suggested an underlying pathology. There was a small contusion on his right leg.

We focused our attention on the more significant injuries – a single bullet entry wound on the right flank, and another wound on the left, just below the rib cage.

"Is this another entry wound or an exit wound?" the pathologist asked, pointing to the wound on the left.

The students were silent for a moment and I racked my own brain to try to recall the difference between the characteristics of an entry and exit wound. My memory came up hazy, and I was relieved when a male student behind me spoke up.

"I think it's an exit wound," he said. "But I'm a little confused by the abrasion around the margin."

The pathologist smiled; the student had quite rightly picked up on the anomaly in this particular wound.

"Well spotted. You wouldn't normally expect that abrasion around an exit wound, which suggests that the victim was probably leaning against something at the point of exit."

I braced myself as the technician came forward to begin the dissection. I'd seen this all before but it felt different now, more brutal somehow. The years away from the medical profession had made me squeamish. I flinched as she made a vertical incision from the sternum right down to the lower abdomen, and we all took an involuntary step backwards as blood oozed out of the abdominal cavity. She quickly scooped it up with a ladle and poured it into a measuring beaker. With the copious amounts of blood she was scooping out, it was clear that he'd bled out into his abdominal cavity. It was no wonder the victim's death came so quickly.

"Could it have been possible to save him?" another student asked.

"That's unlikely," the pathologist answered. "We'll need to document that clearly in our final report. Sometimes family members will come forward saying that their loved one would have survived had the doctors acted more quickly or more aggressively. Our report will show that, with that amount of blood loss, this man didn't stand a chance."

For the first time I was reminded that this was someone's son or brother, not just a gangster. His death meant something to someone.

The students chatted intermittently among themselves as the pathologist continued. He examined each of the abdominal organs in turn, and then removed the organs for further inspection. By now that single bullet's trail of destruction was evident – it tore through the man's right kidney, stomach, pancreas, liver, spleen and diaphragm, before exiting at the left flank.

Two police officers walked in to check on the progress of the autopsy. The pathologist stopped to speak to them, assuring them that the cause of death looked to be straightforward. I noticed that he confined his discussion to the medical findings and I was reminded that this was the extent of his remit.

The students probed him on this when the police officers had left, wanting to understand why he couldn't declare this a murder when it so obviously looked like one. For the first time he stepped out of his role as pathologist, acknowledging the difficulty that he sometimes experienced with needing to confine his findings strictly to the scientific facts in front of him. "It's especially difficult when there is a child lying on the table," he conceded.

To complete the examination the pathologist dissected the lungs, heart and brain, even though there were no obvious signs of damage to them. He was being thorough, making sure to exclude other possible causes of death and to verify that this was an otherwise healthy young man before the gunshot drained the life blood out of him.

The technician spoke for the first time. "Do you want a spare rib, Doctor?" she asked.

He chuckled. "No spare rib for me today, thanks," he said.

They were of course referring to a rib specimen from the corpse. The rest of us laughed as the joke registered. No doubt this was the standard repartee between pathologist and technician when students were in attendance.

When the examination was finally over we stood to the side as the technician put the organs back in the chest and abdominal cavity, doing her best to reconstitute his torso.

"What happens next?" someone asked.

"We submit our findings, and leave the rest up to the courts."

I walked away from the autopsy with a renewed appreciation for the work done at the mortuary and the invaluable contribution it made to the criminal justice system. It was through this meticulous approach and the unbending commitment to uncovering the facts behind unexplained deaths that the truth could be revealed.

How do I begin to examine why my medical career died so young? Will I be as meticulous as I embark on my enquiry? Can I look at the facts of my experiences with clinical detachment, and dissect the various events and motivations? Will I be able to suspend judgement of my actions and the role that external factors played in my decision? Do I have the courage to probe deeply and to ask the questions that I've avoided for all these years?

Perhaps it would be instructive to begin at a place far removed from the white coats and stethoscopes of academic medicine and ask whether there was some underlying pathology that had it doomed from the start.

In the ten years that I was active in the medical profession, first as a student and then as a practising doctor, I was drip-fed death in ever-increasing doses. It was an inescapable occupational hazard of the profession.

From the first day in the anatomy lab I came face to face with death as a grim reality of my work. It was a bloody tumble downhill from there. While it may have been relatively easy to fool myself into thinking that a cadaver was never really human, there was no denying the very real deaths I encountered once I got to the wards. As our clinical training progressed I was confronted with the fact that some patients would never recover from their illnesses or injuries. By the time I graduated I had come to accept death as an integral part of the profession.

But it was one thing to learn about death and quite another to be responsible for preventing it. Community service was that reality check. I had to learn to transform the idealism that still lingered from my student days, and deal with the outcomes I could realistically influence. As one senior doctor put it: "Cure is elusive; the best you can do is to alleviate symptoms. Patients will ultimately die from whatever complaint they are presenting with now, even if it is years down the line."

By the time I completed my community service I knew I'd had my fill. Between the AIDS deaths and people killing each other, I'd seen more death in one year than any person should have to see in a lifetime.

What was I thinking putting myself in the trenches with death and disease? The personal wounds that I'd worked so hard to conceal were too close to the surface, and the level of suffering I was seeing on a daily basis was bound to unravel the armour I had so carefully constructed. My experiences of death in my childhood were my underlying pathology, the Achilles heel that made death in the wards and emergency rooms so difficult to bear.

Coupled with that was the unfortunate timing of my graduation. By the year 2000 HIV had become the leading cause of death in South Africa and, along with chronic diseases, injuries and poverty-related conditions, formed part of the country's so-called quadruple burden of disease. The number of total deaths was on the increase, and it continued to rise until it peaked in 2006. Since then there has been considerable progress in improving the health and life expectancy of the nation, though much still needs to be done. When I started my community service in 2002, I was catching the upsurge of a wave.

Yet, I'd be doing myself an injustice to suggest that the losses of my childhood defeated me. On its own this fact needn't have prevented me from pursuing a medical career. Sure, I may have been flawed going in, but I had so much else going for me. The adversity

I had experienced as a child hadn't broken me; if anything it taught me valuable survival skills and gave me the tenacity not to allow myself to be beaten.

My dream to become a doctor wasn't doomed from the start. And so, as I embark on this journey, the pathologist's process will remain as my guide – to be thorough and systematic. I will also include the stories and experiences of other former doctors to complete my own. Just as a skilled pathologist uses scalpels, probes and other instruments to uncover pathology that may initially be hidden from view, I will use others' stories to shed light on my own.

10 | Cream of the Crop

Recently I had the opportunity to look through my old yearbook from our graduating class. It was full of the usual yearbook entries – pictures from our formal dinner, letters from lecturers and recollections of our experiences over the six years we were all together. A big chunk of the book was dedicated to profiling each student, and we had all been asked the same questions. *What are your best and worst memories of your time at medical school? Where will you be in ten years' time?* That sort of thing.

The one question that intrigued me was: *What would you have studied had you not gone into medicine?* The answers from my classmates were revealing. A significant number of them cited the commercial sector as an alternative, and there were others who mentioned fields as far flung as drama, music and marine biology. What motivates someone to become a doctor when they could just as easily have become a banker? Interestingly the three people who said they would have gone into the arts have since left to pursue their creative dreams.

I was stumped when I read my response: *I can't imagine doing anything else.* Did I really feel that I was perfectly suited to medicine? Had my experiences as a doctor derailed me from my true path? Or did the young student I was then simply lack imagination?

I went looking for answers at the place where many of our dreams were realised. As I drove along Main Road on my way to Groote Schuur Hospital in February 2013 I spotted medical students walking back to their residences and digs. I chuckled at the white coats displayed so prominently over their rucksacks. I use the word *displayed* deliberately; there was no reason, after all, why those coats couldn't be folded up and placed in the students' oversized bags. But there was pride and promise in parading those white coats, a feeling I knew all too well.

Driving there I'd expected the hospital to look different, like returning to your old primary school to find that everything that had once loomed large seemed to have shrunk. But Groote Schuur hadn't shrunk; it stood tall and majestic on the slopes of Devil's Peak, a mere ten minutes' drive from the centre of Cape Town.

As I made my way from the parking lot to the main administrative level at E Floor, I remembered that the different floors and corridors were colour coded, but it didn't help as I'd forgotten how to decipher that code. I didn't trust the little voice inside me, which assured me that I knew this place, so I stopped to ask how to get to the lifts.

Those Groote Schuur lifts were notorious. Stepping into one always felt like I was handing my fate over to the whims of a temperamental demon who resided deep in the bowels of the hospital. My old anxiety reared up again as I stepped into the lift to go up to E Floor, and true to form the elevator started to go down. My fellow passengers and I grumbled and I prayed that we would make it to our destination.

The prolonged ride in the lift gave me a chance to observe my fellow passengers. One I identified by her uniform as someone who worked in the radiology department; the other four looked like patients, probably there for check-ups at the outpatients department. My brain reflexively switched into doctor mode and I wondered what procedure the man standing next to me had undergone. There was a thick dressing on the left side of his neck and I imagined he'd probably had a lymph node removed. I laughed inwardly as I realised that my medical knowledge was now so rusty I couldn't think what else could have happened to him.

I felt more at ease when we finally made it to E Floor. It looked exactly the same as I remembered – the wide, gleaming corridors; patients in blue gowns, some pushing their drip stands next to them as they made their way to the cafeteria; doctors walking in that purposeful way, eyes cast down, deep in thought. The students, on the other hand, sauntered by in small groups; in time they too would learn to put some urgency in their strides.

One thing that was different was Le Grottis, the restaurant where I had come to meet Dr Mark Sonderup, a consultant physician at Groote Schuur and the deputy chairman of the South African Medical Association. Back in my student days we only had a cafeteria where we could buy some basic takeaways; this fully fledged restaurant was certainly an improvement.

I walked into Le Grottis to find doctors sitting in groups at a number of tables, talking and laughing over coffee and some eats. I felt self-conscious. Was it written on my face that I had turned my back on the profession? Could the other doctors tell that I didn't really belong there any more?

I chose a table at the far end of the restaurant; I wanted a quiet space where I could question Mark about some of the issues affecting doctors in the public sector. I remembered him from my community service year at Jooste; he was a registrar then, training to be a specialist physician. We worked together briefly in the medical ward and if he was still anything like he had been then I knew he wouldn't hold back on expressing his opinion.

He didn't see me at first so I watched him for a few seconds as he scanned the room. The ten years since I'd last seen him hadn't aged him at all. His blond hair was still cropped short, giving his face a youthful appearance that was enhanced by his bright, darting eyes. He was dressed casually in chinos and a checked short-sleeved shirt – no white coat; his stethoscope hung loosely around his neck. He smiled when he spotted me, and when he walked towards me I couldn't help noticing the unmistakable swagger of someone who had reached the pinnacle of his career.

He began by asking me a question, which threw me a bit. "Why did you study medicine in the first place?"

I hesitated for a second, and then I realised what a skilled clinician he was. He knew how to get to the heart of the matter in seconds.

"It was aspirational," I said, aware that my response was a little vague. I had come to interview him, after all, so I didn't expect to be interrogated.

My response may have been clumsy, but there was truth in it nonetheless. In many ways my motivation *was* aspirational – I wanted to make a difference, to cure people, to better my own life. When you come from a home where you are told in drunken rants that you are nobody, you either start believing the insults or you fight to prove your worth. I fought. With the wisdom that the intervening years had bestowed, I also realised that on some level I wanted to acquire the tools to defeat death.

I said none of this out loud so perhaps he wasn't satisfied with my brief response. His brow furrowed momentarily and when he spoke again I felt as if I was being lectured to. "Too often people want to get into medicine for the wrong reasons. I think it's important that prospective students are very clear about the decision they are making," he said.

I challenged him. "How clear can an eighteen-year-old be about anything, though?"

His face softened a little. "Fair enough," he conceded, "but they must at least get some fundamentals straight. As a start they need to forget everything they've seen on *Grey's Anatomy* and all the other television dramas that glamourise medicine."

I laughed out loud. In my day it was *Doogie Howser, M.D.* that had made being a doctor look like a fun pastime.

Mark had struck a nerve. I had to acknowledge that on some level I was seduced by what it would mean to be a doctor. Or at least what I imagined it would mean. When I was growing up the doctors in our community were the first citizens, the people everyone else looked up to. They had the big houses, the fancy cars and the prestige that so many coveted. They were the ones who had broken through the limitations of being black in apartheid South Africa.

I was not alone in my desire for personal advancement, and it had no racial bias. When I was a student a common topic of discussion among my peers was the value of the UCT medical degree. Many were concerned about how the changes to medical training that the government was proposing would affect the international status of our qualification as they were already eyeing lucrative posts in overseas markets. Today around a third of my graduating class is working abroad, mostly in the United Kingdom.

Mark steered my thoughts back to medical students. "I think we need to make sure that students know what they are committing to when they decide to get into this profession. Believe me, that's the one thing that's going to keep them sane at three o'clock in the morning when they've been on call for 24 hours."

I agreed with him, but I also questioned whether the right kinds of people were being recruited into medical schools in the first place. After all, it was the straight-A students who made it in, and they may be too ambitious for public service.

"It's a moving target," he said.

I frowned, so he continued. "What makes a good doctor today isn't necessarily what will make a good doctor in 30 years' time. Our society's needs will change and we will need to adapt to those changes, but a few fundamentals will remain the same."

"And what are those?" I asked.

"We need people with solid ability, good character and fortitude."

"But surely they don't need to have straight As? Are we not missing potentially good candidates by focusing too strongly on academic results? Should we not at least interview prospective students before accepting them? There were a number of people in my class who probably wouldn't have been allowed in had someone interviewed them."

Mark sniggered. "I know what you mean," he said. "But remember, not everyone is going to end up on the frontline, interacting with patients. We do still need people who will go into research and other areas of academia. Besides, how do you objectively determine whether someone will make a good doctor? The system that we have now is a good-enough approximation."

I was not convinced that that was enough. In their article titled "Fit for Purpose? The appropriate education of health professionals in South Africa"[1] professors Vanessa Burch and Steve Reid, specialists at UCT's faculty of health sciences, highlighted the need for more concerted efforts to address the gross shortages of health care personnel in the public sector, especially in the rural areas. They asserted that more attention needed to be given to the kinds of students who were being selected, particularly as research had shown that students who came from rural areas and disadvantaged communities were more likely to return to those communities when they qualified.

Mark didn't think the problem lay with the recruitment process, though he acknowledged that it was part of the equation. For me, the kind of people recruited into the profession was an important consideration.

I was reminded of my conversation with Mark a few days later when I spoke to Vongai*. I had found her via a fortuitous email that arrived in my inbox. She was a member of an online discussion forum. Ordinarily that kind of email would have been deleted, but my interest was piqued when I saw the title in front of her name. I was further intrigued when I clicked to view her profile – a medical doctor

---

1 Reid, Steve and Burch, Vanessa. "Fit for purpose? The appropriate education of health professionals in South Africa" in *South African Medical Journal*, [S.l.], v. 101, n. 1, pp. 25-26, January 2011. ISSN 2078-5135.

who had left the profession and was now a Japanese-to-English and German-to-English medical translator. I immediately arranged a phone interview and we spoke over Skype a few days later.

By her own admission Vongai was a nerd as a child. When other children were playing outside she preferred to tinker with her computer, teaching herself the ins and outs of computer programming. The language of technology was second nature to her, and in many ways she found this language easier than communicating with human beings.

Vongai was born in Zimbabwe to an engineer father and teacher mother. Her family moved to the South African town of Rustenburg in the North West province when she was three years old. The young Vongai displayed an uncanny ease with machinery.

She laughed as she recalled one of her earliest memories. "One day when my parents were out I dismantled the VCR because I wanted to see where the pictures came from. When they returned to find a heap of wires on the living room floor, I was sure I would be in trouble. But after the initial shock they were impressed with what I had done. From then on I was given all sorts of electrical appliances to play with."

She thrived on a challenge and was always pushing herself to learn and achieve more. Her interest in computers was a natural extension of her intellectual curiosity. When the time came for her to choose her future career, medicine – which was so unlike the computers that had become her familiar companions – seemed like the right kind of challenge. She was accepted to UCT Medical School in 2000.

As it turned out, studying medicine wasn't as difficult as she had hoped. She seldom attended lectures, electing instead to spend most of her time at university holed up in her dormitory room, tapping away at her computer. She even found the time to teach herself Japanese online, a feat more in keeping with her quest for intellectual stimulation. She easily passed her exams and graduated in 2005.

It was only when she began her internship at Rustenburg Provincial Hospital that for the first time in her life Vongai was confronted with something she didn't excel at. "I realised that just because you are trained in something doesn't mean you'll be good at it," she said.

"What exactly was the difficulty for you?" I asked.

"I struggled with the volume of patients I was seeing on a daily basis. Rustenburg has a large mining population, and with this comes alcohol abuse, domestic violence and an enormous amount of HIV. We were trained to put patients first, but the sheer numbers made this task impossible."

I asked when she knew she would leave the profession. She chuckled, "I knew when I was studying that I would probably leave at some point, but I figured I'd already come this far I might as well continue. When the push came it was easy for me to make the decision."

"What was the push?" I asked.

The exuberance she'd displayed thus far in our conversation became subdued. "The nurses' strike in 2007. It was awful," she said.

I wanted to know more, and her voice was tinged with sadness as she recalled that troubled time.

"All the clinics were closed so patients came flooding through to the hospital. The doctors were swamped; we were doing our own work plus the nursing duties as well. We were struggling to cope, and at one point things turned nasty as people were so exhausted they were threatening to leave the hospital and turn off their phones. No one wanted to be there; we'd all had enough. That strike was the breaking point for me. I had to get out, and when I finished my community service at the end of that year, I left for good."

Vongai went on to work in IT consulting at the global management consulting firm, Accenture. She was good at it, and she enjoyed her work. She was back to tinkering with her computers.

I couldn't help thinking that Vongai probably shouldn't have gone into the medical profession in the first place, that she wasn't fit for the purpose of practising medicine. But she was a brilliant student so she easily fulfilled the admission requirements. It is sometimes said that we are victims of the exams we pass.

I continued my enquiry into medical education when I met with Professor James Volmink, dean of the faculty of health sciences at the University of Stellenbosch, a week later. It was my first visit to the Stellenbosch medical campus and when I arrived a part of me felt like I was entering rival territory.

Professor Volmink was no rival, though. I'd expected him to look like the quintessential professor with unkempt hair and dishevelled clothes, so I was pleasantly surprised to be greeted by a tall, slender man dressed smartly in tailored suit trousers and a cuffed shirt. He was warm and welcoming, and I immediately felt at ease as we settled into the couches in his spacious office.

Like me, Professor Volmink was a UCT graduate, though he qualified at a time when the odds were heavily stacked against a black person making it in the overwhelmingly white profession. He studied at UCT in the late seventies, and was one of only five students of colour in his class of more than 180. As students in a segregated South Africa, they were not allowed to examine white patients, attend autopsies on white corpses or even dissect white cadavers. They were also excluded from participating in the university's cultural, sporting or social activities. Theirs was just to turn up for lectures and to do as they were told.

"Stellenbosch was worse," he added. "They refused to accept me here when I wanted to pursue my postgraduate studies."

"It's a monumental achievement, then, that you are now dean of faculty," I said.

He smiled. "Change is inevitable. Good leadership is about having the courage to cause that change."

I wanted to know whether enough was being done to recruit students who were committed to public service. I mentioned Burch and Reid's article and he nodded his agreement, detailing the measures that Stellenbosch had taken to produce doctors who were fit for purpose.

Every year the university revises its selection criteria, placing considerable emphasis on applicants' non-academic attributes such as leadership qualities, sporting achievements and involvement in community initiatives. They too recognise the importance of the well-rounded doctor. In addition the university had established a rural training facility in Worcester in the Cape Winelands district where students were given the opportunity to experience rural medicine during their training.

I was heartened by the efforts the university was making, and I hoped in time those interventions would translate into more doctors working in the areas where they were most needed. I was also painfully aware of the role that I, and others like me, had played in contributing to the shortage of doctors.

Perhaps with his wisdom Professor Volmink could see the large stick I'd been beating myself with over the years. "Remember that doctors are human beings. A few years ago I attended my 25-year reunion at medical school. A significant proportion of the class was in attendance, and I would estimate that about 80 per cent of them were based overseas," he said.

He paused and smiled warmly. "We are all on a journey, and sometimes that journey takes us overseas, into the private sector or even out of the profession altogether. People have got to be allowed to take that journey."

I returned his smile. I was grateful for his words.

I had good intentions; I readily acknowledge that. But was it enough to mean well? Was I fit for purpose? In all honesty I believe that in many ways I was. I was a conscientious student and a good doctor. I cared deeply and I wanted to make a difference. I realise now that this has been a source of deep internal conflict for me over the years – this knowing that I hadn't made a mistake by pursuing a medical career in the first place, yet also feeling that I'd made the correct decision by choosing to leave.

Had I chosen to stay I would probably have chosen a specialisation in internal medicine, with particular focus on HIV. And I would have made a success of it. But at what cost?

11 | Baptism of Fire

When I started looking for other doctors who had left the medical profession I wondered what I would encounter, how similar – or not – their stories would be to my own. Intuitively I knew that my experiences weren't unique to me, though back then we never talked about what we were going through. The profession didn't lend itself to the sharing of hardship; we were all high achievers who knew how to soldier on.

I was introduced to Nina* by a mutual friend who described her as a disgruntled intern, rearing to get out. I was curious to hear what could be causing such distress to a recently qualified doctor.

I was pleasantly surprised when I met Nina. She had warned me that she'd be post-call so I was expecting to meet a weary doctor with drawn features, bloodshot eyes and clothes in desperate need of a change. Instead I encountered a stylish woman in her mid-twenties, casually dressed in royal-blue slim-fit pants and a tan T-shirt. Her chestnut-brown hair was held up in a fashionably messy chignon, with loose tendrils framing a pretty, round face with an immaculate olive complexion. She looked almost carefree, except her eyes gave me a glimpse into the turmoil that was raging inside her.

She didn't waste time with pleasantries as we took our places at a table at the far end of a busy coffee shop in the upmarket suburb of

Newlands. I felt uncomfortable sitting so close to the other patrons given the nature of the conversation we were about to have. If she was concerned she didn't let on. She seemed eager to offload, so I sat back and let her speak.

Nina was born and raised in KwaZulu-Natal, the gifted daughter of Dutch immigrant parents. She excelled at school, earning the admiration and praise of her peers and teachers. She was creatively inclined and was inspired by her artist mother, but when the time came for her to choose a field of study after finishing school she went for what she considered a "safe bet".

"There is no security in art. I saw how much my mother struggled; it was great when she made a sale but tough when she didn't for months at a time. I didn't want that for my own life," she said. There was a hint of sadness in her voice as she spoke and I wondered whether this was a decision she had tried to justify to herself many times over.

Nina enrolled at Stellenbosch University and by her own admission she found her time there challenging.

"It's not that the work was difficult. I just struggled with the way in which we were taught. The consultants and registrars were constantly assessing us and we were frequently humiliated in public. The pressure was unbearable sometimes."

I knew that practice well. "It is an integral part of the culture of large teaching institutions," I said, mainly to reassure her.

In addition to the demands of her studies Nina craved the creative expression that art had given her but she found little time to feed that yearning. In time she began to falter.

The signs were subtle at first. She was miserable, not enjoying her life at university and anxious about being assessed. It was only when she became forgetful and started making mistakes – behaviour that was inconsistent with her focused and meticulous nature – that she knew that something was seriously wrong.

"I was diagnosed with depression and placed on medication. The misery lifted and I was able to focus on my work again, but I still found it difficult to cope. I really don't know how I managed to pass my exams given all that was going on."

When she graduated in 2010 it was a testament to her fighting spirit and her determination to make more of her life than her mother had. That same spirit was put to the test again when she began her internship in January 2011.

In 2008 the compulsory year of internship for new medical graduates was increased to two years. This move was in recognition of the fact that trainee doctors needed a longer time to adjust to the demands and responsibilities of their new position. The additional year was also intended to give the new doctors broader exposure to the various disciplines, and it became a requirement of their internship that they rotate through the essential disciplines of internal medicine, obstetrics and gynaecology, paediatrics, surgery and family medicine. Previously intern rotations were determined largely by where the doctors were based; it was not unusual for some to get through their internship training having only gained experience in two or three disciplines.

Nina rotated between Groote Schuur, Red Cross and Mowbray Maternity hospitals, as well as the Hanover Park Community Health Centre, and she found the demands of being a junior doctor overwhelming. In a typical month she worked, on average, six days on call, on which days she began work at seven o'clock in the morning and worked right through the night until seven the following morning. On a relatively quiet night she would get a few hours' sleep, but those opportunities were few and far between. Likewise meal breaks were little more than hastily wolfed-down sandwiches if the time allowed. The day after her call she could leave when the ward round was finished and any urgent duties were completed, usually around mid-morning.

Nina's working hours were not unusual. Junior doctors are required to work up to 20 hours' overtime per week, in addition to the 40 hours of regular working time. In its guidelines on internship training the Health Professions Council further stipulates that interns should work in hospitals accredited for internship training under the supervision of suitably trained and experienced doctors. It is the intention that internship training should equip newly qualified doctors with the skills and experience that will enable them to practise independently in the future. Unfortunately, though they are not meant to serve as extra hands in the public health system, interns sometimes become the backbone of the staff complement in public health facilities.

When I'd asked Mark Sonderup about the quality of internship training he was unequivocal in his response. "The Health Professions Council has been charged with the responsibility of overseeing internship training. It is part of their mandate to accredit hospitals for training, and to ensure that such training does indeed occur at these accredited institutions."

"Is this responsibility being effectively discharged?" I asked.

He shrugged. "The fact is, they have the power to do it. They may say that they don't always have the capacity, but that's a different matter. They cannot renege on this mandate. If an intern feels that they are being unduly exploited, then they can report it."

"What recourse is there? Is this mandate even enforceable?"

Mark was insistent. "Accreditation can be withdrawn from the particular hospital. We all know that many hospitals cannot survive without interns, so action will be taken."

Indeed, many hospitals can't survive without interns. But isn't this part of the problem?

Nicolette Erasmus, an attorney with a special interest in the medical profession, wrote a scathing article in the *South African Medical Journal*[2] in June 2012, in which she criticised the working hours of junior doctors, even going as far as to liken them to a form of slave labour. In the article she claimed that interns and community service doctors were exploited by the state in order to bolster an under-resourced public health care system. Furthermore the fact that the doctors were required to work extended hours – only a portion of which was paid – in order to qualify to practise medicine in South Africa gave them very little choice in the matter. She didn't pull any punches: "No other profession in this country is subject to the level of coercion and exploitation by the state to which medical interns and community service doctors are exposed. The Minister of Health must act decisively against human rights abuses to regain the moral high ground."

When I read the article I found myself feeling quite conflicted.

2 Erasmus, Nicolette. "Slaves of the state – medical internship and community service in South Africa" in *South African Medical Journal*, [S.l.], v. 102, n. 8, pp. 655-658, June 2012. ISSN 2078-5135.

Though I knew that much of what she was saying was true, I wanted to protest, to tell her that she didn't know what she was talking about. How could an "outsider" like her possibly understand? The demands of the profession necessitated a way of working that was unique to "us". But I realised that this oddity was exactly the point she was making. Why was it that doctors worked these ludicrous hours that made no sense legally or rationally? As a signatory to a host of human rights and labour laws, South Africa had committed itself to a society where the rights of its citizens were protected and where undue exploitation was prohibited. What justification could there be for excluding junior doctors from this protection?

Labour law aside, working long hours with little sleep or rest was just dangerous. I cannot count the number of times I walked onto a ward after a night on call and completely forgot why I was there. I'd stand at the entrance, mining my exhausted brain for clues, only to come up with more questions than answers. Thankfully I made no serious mistakes on those hazy post-call mornings, but that was more a matter of luck than design.

"The senior doctors don't understand," Nina continued. "Their attitude seems to be – we did it, now you must too. But the challenges that we face now are very different to the ones they had to deal with."

She was right, of course. The burden of disease in the South African health sector had seen a massive explosion since the advent of HIV. The disease radically altered the demands placed on health care professionals.

For Nina the demands made on her time, energy and wellbeing were overwhelming. "It's not just the long hours and the workload that we have to deal with. We are also required to make life-and-death decisions, and frankly as junior doctors we are simply not equipped to make them."

I interrupted her for the first time. "But surely internship is necessary? At some point you've got to take on the responsibility of being a doctor," I said.

"I agree," she snapped back. "I have no problem with internship per se. It's the degree of responsibility that bothers me."

I knew what she meant. There were few things more terrifying than being summoned to the ward on a night on call to tend to a critically ill patient. Of course you knew what there was to do; in theory anyway. Given a less stressful situation you could probably formulate a plan of action for the particular crisis and execute it successfully. But logical thinking and problem-solving skills were elusive in those terrifying moments; you had to think on your feet and take decisive action. The magnitude of the decisions – and the potential for doing harm – was enormous. In the commercial arena this would be the equivalent of allowing a recent commerce graduate to take responsibility for decisions that could financially cripple the company.

"And some decisions are just out of our scope of expertise," Nine continued. "How am I supposed to help when a patient has lost his ID document or when a female patient wants to lay charges against her abusive husband?"

For Nina, it was the sense of helplessness that bothered her most, the feeling that in spite of her world-class education she was often unable to provide what her patients really needed. She should have completed her internship at the end of 2012 but her time was interrupted when, halfway through the second year, she suffered another breakdown, which necessitated that she take a leave of absence for six months.

As Nina continued talking I grew increasingly uncomfortable. She was angry, disillusioned and bitter, lambasting the profession for what she felt were its failings. I stopped to consider my reaction and I realised that the awkwardness arose from the mirror she was putting up to my own feelings. She was in the same space I was at the end of my community service. I wasn't depressed as Nina had been, but I can't say I was perfectly well either. I was disillusioned, traumatised and desperate to leave a profession that had failed to live up to my expectations. Or perhaps I'd failed to live up to my own expectations of what it meant to be a doctor. This was meant to be my chance to make a difference and to heal people, yet it became increasingly clear that much of what I was doing was alleviating symptoms. In addition my own life was in disarray as I spent most of my time either working or recovering from work.

Nina planned to leave the medical profession after completing her internship. She had already secured a job working as a general manager for an educational NGO, an opportunity she relished as she hoped it would allow her the opportunity to make a difference in the way she felt she couldn't as a doctor.

For years the South African health sector has been haemorrhaging doctors – to overseas markets, the private sector and through sideways shifts to academia, medical aid schemes and the pharmaceutical industry. This is the question that has lingered over the years – to what extent did practising medicine in South Africa at that time contribute to my decision to leave the medical profession? Would it have been different had I practised elsewhere, at another time, under different circumstances? What is driving us away from the places where we are most needed – public-sector hospitals and clinics across South Africa?

Undeniably the environment in which doctors in this country operate presents a unique set of challenges. For one doctor the demands of her work and the nature of the decisions she was required to make left her feeling like she was playing God with people's lives.

I met with Wanda* at a coffee shop at the V&A Waterfront in Cape Town, a short distance from the financial services corporation where she works. I didn't know what to expect; I'd been referred to her by an acquaintance and we had only ever exchanged email communication. All I knew was that she was a former doctor from the Cape Flats who had left the profession to pursue interests in financial services.

She started talking as soon as we sat down. She was bubbly and animated; I liked her instantly. Wanda was her family's golden child, the one whose intellect had shown them the possibility of having a doctor in the family. They'd encouraged her to apply to medical school and when she was accepted at UCT in 1999 it was the realisation of her family's dream.

"How did you feel about studying?" I asked as we sat drinking our coffees.

"It was great, actually. I enjoyed the science of medicine. It was like putting together clues to get to what was ailing the patient," she said.

"So what went wrong?" I asked.

"It was a gradual realisation," she said. When Wanda reached fourth year at medical school she felt uncomfortable about examining patients.

This revelation surprised me. She came across as such an extrovert, a "people person", so it seemed odd that she would have felt that way.

"It wasn't the patients per se," she explained. "If anything I felt sorry for them. Here they were, gravely ill in a tertiary hospital, and they had to endure groups of doctors and students prodding them from time to time. It didn't feel right for me."

"And yet you continued with your studies?"

"Yes, I continued. One of our tutors assured us that we all had a place in the profession, that in time we would find that place and we would stay there and make a valuable contribution. I believed him."

Wanda hadn't found her place by the time she graduated in 2004. She took up an intern post at Tygerberg Hospital in the northern suburbs of Cape Town. Like Groote Schuur, Tygerberg is a tertiary teaching hospital. However, in Wanda's eyes, the two hospitals had little in common.

"Groote Schuur was like a five-star hotel compared to Tygerberg. I would joke with my colleagues that I would rather die than be treated at Tygerberg. I made them promise to drive me to Groote Schuur on the other side of the city if I ever fell ill on duty."

Wanda started her internship rotation in ear, nose and throat (ENT) surgery, and she was thrown in the deep end with little support and limited resources.

"We frequently had paediatric patients, but there was no blood-taking equipment suitable for use on children in the ENT ward. I had to go to the paediatric ward and beg the nurses for tubes, and they were reluctant to part with their supplies. No one taught me this at med school – what to do when there's no equipment."

Wanda came to realise that there was a lot she wasn't taught at medical school. Furthermore as a junior doctor she had limited access to more experienced doctors who could help to fill the gaps in her knowledge. "Internship is meant to be the time when you learn how to do, but at no point does anyone show you what to do. You are expected to just get on with it."

"See one, do one, teach one, right?" I said.

"Exactly," she replied. "Except I didn't even get the chance to see one."

Wanda relied on printed-out notes and some guidance from the nursing staff to teach her the procedures that she was meant to perform. It was trial and error, but she eventually got the knack of it. She became very competent at removing foreign objects from ears, cauterising bleeding noses, and draining collections of pus at the back of the throat.

Listening to Wanda speak, I was struck by the fact that, as a student, I didn't think to question the *see one, do one, teach one* approach to our training. I accepted it as the way things had always been done. It was only when I started practising as a doctor that I came to appreciate how inadequate it was. What level of competence can possibly be gained from observing a procedure once before being deemed fit enough to perform it and then in turn teach it? Not only was it nerve-racking for the inexperienced doctor, it was potentially dangerous for the patient. Imagine being on the receiving end of a procedure being carried out by a junior doctor who had only ever seen it performed once? Or, in Wanda's case, a doctor who had relied on a piece of paper for guidance?

The disenchantment that had been creeping in came to a head during her paediatrics rotation, and eventually led to the realisation that she no longer wanted to practise medicine. When she was on call she was required to work in theatre, resuscitating babies who had been born by Caesarean section. Often these resuscitations required intubation – inserting a breathing tube into the airway. She had only ever attempted an intubation once before as a student.

"That one attempt in sixth year wasn't successful, so I really didn't know what I was doing. Now my job involved intubating babies in theatre," she said. Understandably she was terrified.

One night in theatre was particularly traumatic. "It was simultaneously the best and the worst day of my career," she said. I urged her to explain.

"Two babies needed resuscitating in quick succession. Despite the fact that I didn't have much experience, I was successful in both cases. I saved those babies. I know that they would have died had I not done what I did," she said.

"What was the dreadful bit, then?" I asked.

"I wasn't sure I should have done it. Both the babies were born to HIV-positive mothers, one of whom was in critical condition and the other seriously ill with TB. Those women wouldn't be around much longer to look after their babies."

She burst into tears as she told her husband about it the next morning. He was at a loss as to how to comfort her. "He kept trying to tell me that I'd done well, but I wasn't buying it. I couldn't fully articulate why I felt so terrible. What did I save them for?"

Her husband was the voice of reason, telling her that she couldn't foresee what would happen; maybe those children would have great lives, be cared for by loving family members and grow up to make something of their lives.

Wanda didn't agree. "They came from very poor circumstances. It's conceivable, I guess, that they could have gone on to have wonderful lives, but the chances were far greater that they were facing misery. I sentenced those children to a life I wouldn't choose for myself."

Wanda was echoing a sentiment I encountered often during my career. Like her I didn't feel that the ethics lectures we had at medical school did enough to equip us for the magnitude of the decisions we were confronted with in the field. South Africa faces major challenges in the provision of health care. The existence of great need in the context of limited resources meant that the decisions we made were not only based on clinical imperatives, but also had to take into account patients' circumstances and the resource constraints in the health system.

There were times when I struggled with ethical dilemmas, particularly when limited resources were made available to patients who had made it clear they didn't want them. When I worked at Jooste we often saw patients who had attempted suicide. Most of them weren't serious attempts – patients who had taken a handful of oral contraceptives or a few diuretics. Though these so-called parasuicides were not serious in themselves, they were red flags that indicated that successful attempts could occur in future. For me, though, it was the more serious attempts that bothered me for the ethical dilemma they posed.

The patients would be rushed into the resuscitation cubicle after they had taken a sizeable cocktail of drugs, often washed down with copious amounts of alcohol. I felt sorry for them as we rushed to re-suscitate them and drag them back from their self-imposed stupor. How utterly demoralising it must be for patients to put so much effort into trying to kill themselves, only to wake up to find a bunch of doctors and nurses doing their best to reverse all that work. Another thing they'd failed at. They had taken the decision to end their lives; what right did we have to invalidate that decision? I knew that my responsibility as a doctor was to treat them when they were in my emergency room, but it just didn't seem right to pour resources into people who had chosen to take their own lives, and yet patients with HIV who desperately wanted to live were de-nied life-saving treatment.

When Wanda's internship ended she resigned from Tygerberg and didn't take up a community service post. "I decided that other people could try to save the babies. I wanted to rather be the one who helps them to have a better life."

Her family was angered by her decision, and many people in her community criticised her, some going as far as to call her selfish and ungrateful. She was unrepentant. "I was tired of playing God with people's lives."

Once out of the profession Wanda drifted for a number of years before she found work that appealed to her. She was offered a job as an analyst at a financial services company, where she has been for five years. She has evolved her role over the years to focus on investor education.

"I am passionate about educating people about finances. At the end of the day you can help people to live longer and you can help more people to live, but money improves the quality of their lives. I want to be on the happy end of life, not the survival end. Practising medicine in the public sector was like scooping water out of a sinking ship. You just couldn't win."

Though I agree with Wanda that money makes a huge difference to one's quality of life, in medicine money isn't everything. Even in a resource-rich country like England we still needed to make difficult end-of-life decisions. I remember one night on call being summoned to see an old man in the medical ward. He had a fever and his right leg was red, swollen and painful. I treated him aggressively with intravenous antibiotics. The next morning the infection on the patient's leg showed marked improvement, but the doctor in charge wasn't impressed.

"For goodness' sake, don't rush in to treat," he admonished after we'd assessed the patient. Just because the resources were available didn't mean they had be used in every case. At some point the decision needed to be made to let nature take its course.

12 | A Different Kind of Service

I could relate to Nina and Wanda's feeling that they could only make a difference in people's lives outside the medical profession. I too had felt that my efforts were ineffectual, though I still felt guilty for walking away. News reports on the dire shortage of health care personnel in the health sector would trigger intense feelings of shame about the seemingly selfish decision I had made.

A friend of mine, himself a former doctor, recently offered a more empowering perspective. In his view, the intimate exposure, which we were given through our training and practice, to the hardships experienced by many South Africans was the foundation upon which we could find ways to have a positive impact, whether from within the profession or outside of it. We had seen people at their most vulnerable and disenfranchised. It was impossible to forget that or to pretend that these circumstances didn't exist.

I was intrigued by the way one doctor has chosen to use her medical training to carve out a niche in the world of fashion and apparel. She has not only found a way to express her creativity, but she is also making a difference in her particular way.

Yolisa* is a medical doctor who is combining her love of fashion with her clinical skills in an innovative business. I'd read about her in a glamorous women's magazine and as we spoke over the phone

I imagined that she was immaculately groomed and stylishly dressed, in line with the upmarket and sophisticated image of her lingerie boutique. Yolisa started the business in 2012 after a less-than-inspiring time in private practice.

She grew up in the Eastern Cape and after matriculating in 1993 she pursued a medical degree at the University of KwaZulu-Natal. Yolisa began her medical career as an intern at Livingstone Hospital in Port Elizabeth before moving on to Cecilia Makiwane Hospital in the township of Mdantsane for community service. She later worked at a government-funded ARV clinic. Though the early years were typically challenging, she enjoyed her work. "I was making a difference, and I found it rewarding."

"So why did you leave?" I asked.

She giggled. "The bright city lights called," she said.

Yolisa moved to Johannesburg where she was dazzled by the fast-paced lifestyle and the seemingly endless opportunities. Her life as a doctor seemed dull in comparison. At the time she was doing GP locum jobs and she found the work monotonous and uninspiring. She moved on to a medical advisory role in an insurance company, but there was little improvement in job satisfaction.

"It was all the same. I felt like a glorified clerk. There was no real challenge; I was seeing minor complaints and filling in forms. After a while I became restless. On top of that I felt undervalued by the powers that be."

Yolisa decided to make a break. "I realised that, in the work I was doing, I was keeping one foot in the profession and it wasn't doing me any good," she said.

"A sideways shift," I added.

"Exactly. I had to jump, and either sink or swim. It was terrifying but I knew that I had to do it. So in 2010 I started running."

I burst out laughing. "Running out of the profession?" I asked, bemused.

She joined in my laughter. "I started road running, but I guess in a way I was also running out of the profession. I was training hard and when I completed the New York Marathon in November 2011 I knew that, if I could accomplish that, I could do anything. So I left." The confidence that she gained from finishing the marathon gave her the courage to take a giant leap to start her own business.

I was curious about her choice of venture. "Why a lingerie boutique?"

She chuckled. "Many people have wondered about that. Some people back at home even went as far as to ask why I would give up being a doctor to sell panties. It makes perfect sense to me, though. My mother died of cervical cancer, so women's health is very close to my heart. I wanted to create something that would help to restore women's self-esteem and to have a positive impact on their body image."

Yolisa's boutique caters for fuller-figured women and those who have undergone mastectomies. She sells breast prostheses and mastectomy bras, and the business also affords her the opportunity to educate women about their health.

Yolisa's lingerie boutique is certainly a unique way of using her medical training, and it emphasised the pattern I'd seen emerging from my interviews – the calling to make a difference lingers in many of us, even if it finds expression in vastly different forms.

Not only has the world beyond medicine opened up spectacularly in recent years, but even within the medical field people are starting to put a unique signature on the way they choose to make that difference.

Then there's Riaad Moosa, comedian, actor and former doctor. Before I met him, I assumed I knew how Riaad's story would go. From my preliminary research I gathered that both his parents are doctors – his mother a general practitioner and his father an orthopaedic surgeon – and that his sister had completed her medical studies at UCT in 2012 and was in her first year of internship. Based on this clearly medical family background, I imagined that Riaad had followed the path that was expected of him, setting aside his love of comedy to follow in the family tradition.

We were sitting at the Oakhurst Farmstall in the Cape Town suburb of Kenilworth, just a short distance away from where both our children are at school. I'd arrived before him and had formulated my hypothesis as I'd sat waiting. I tailored my questions to fit the hypothesis, expecting to hear a story of family conflict and his eventual defiance of his family's expectations in order to follow his dream.

When I saw him walking towards the café I was struck by how young he looked dressed in jeans and a casual T-shirt, slinging a rucksack over his back. I noticed one of the ladies in the shop smile at him broadly when he walked in. I wondered whether she recognised him; his stand-up comedy shows had earned him a considerable level of national celebrity. Or perhaps she was just responding to his fresh-faced good looks.

When we started speaking he was reserved, shy almost, and at first it was difficult for me to reconcile his unassuming manner with the successful comedian and actor he had become.

I began by sharing my hypothesis with him.

He was quick to set me straight. "Stand-up comedy wasn't even on my radar when I was growing up. I didn't know about it. I always wanted to be a doctor," he said.

I was surprised by this revelation. "Comedy was quite a dramatic shift, then, wasn't it?" I asked.

He shrugged. "I guess so, but I always liked to do impersonations. As a child I was quite reserved, but I would gravitate towards the dramatic whenever we were required to give a speech in class."

I set aside my notes along with my hypothesis. "So when did the introduction to comedy come?"

"It started with magic, actually. When I was in Standard Seven[3] a friend of mine showed me a pamphlet for the College of Magic in Lansdowne. He was keen to enrol and he invited me to go with him."

"Did you go?"

"Yes, I did go. But my friend's parents didn't allow him to." He chortled. "And now he's in IT." His tone lightened a little as he said this and for a second I glimpsed Riaad the comedian. Just as quickly he became serious again. "Magic is considered *haram* in Islam."

"So how come you were allowed to go?" I wondered.

"It's the occult stuff that is *haram*. These were just innocent tricks we were taught for the purpose of entertainment. There was nothing sinister about it."

Over time Riaad's magic tricks took on a more comedic slant,

---

3 Standard Seven (now called Grade Nine) is the ninth year of education in the South African school system.

though sometimes unintentionally so. "I took part in a magic competition when I was in Standard Nine[4], and one of the acts was to make a spherical orb float across the stage. The orb was attached to wires, of course, but with the correct positioning of the lighting you couldn't see them. It worked brilliantly during rehearsal."

He paused briefly and smiled; I returned the smile, anticipating a disaster. "We hadn't expected that on the day of the competition people would bring flash cameras to the show. Our oversight was made painfully obvious when the flashes gave the trick away and several bitterly disappointed children started screaming, 'The wires, the wires,' when I was halfway through my act. Needless to say I didn't do well in that competition."

Riaad continued his magic while he finished school and would perform at children's birthday parties in order to earn pocket money. Magic remained a part of his life even when he enrolled at UCT Medical School to pursue his dream of becoming a doctor.

One night when he was in his fourth year of study he went to a comedy show for the first time. "It was incredible. I'd never experienced anything like it; I was hooked."

"Did you know then that you would become a comedian?" I asked, thinking that this had been his epiphany moment.

"Not at all. At least it didn't occur that way on a conscious level. All I knew was that I had discovered something that really appealed to me. I was curious."

His curiosity drove him to take a year out of medical school to explore this new-found love. His family was supportive, though others in his close-knit community openly questioned his decision.

4 Standard Nine (now Grade Eleven) is the eleventh year of education.

During that year off Riaad immersed himself in comedy, an experience he found exhilarating. He began to associate with other comedians, attended numerous shows and he learned the craft. Initially he performed comedy magic, but by the end of that year he had discarded magic altogether to concentrate on stand-up comedy. He was in his element.

When the time came for him to return to medical school, he did so happily. He was still committed to his original plan, and he went on to graduate at the end of 2001. It was a proud moment for him and his family.

I wondered whether he felt conflicted in any way during this time, torn between two passions.

He shook his head. "No, I didn't. I was just living my life each day, doing the things that mattered to me. I guess circumstances nudged me towards comedy because I loved it so much. I was instinctively pulled towards it."

"Was there a push out of medicine at all?"

He didn't hesitate. "Of course. Internship and community service were an onslaught on every level – physically, emotionally and mentally. The things I feel worst about in my life happened in those two years."

Riaad was based at Natalspruit Hospital during his internship and returned to Cape Town for his community service, where he was based first at Site B Community Health Centre in Khayelitsha then Groote Schuur Hospital. It was a harrowing time for him, particularly the first few months at Natalspruit. Like so many, he found himself entrusted with an enormous responsibility but given little guidance on how to discharge it.

He looked off into the distance as he recalled an incident during that first year. The medical officers who were meant to be supervising the newly qualified interns were themselves overextended, and an informal arrangement was agreed where the interns and MOs split the shifts in order to give each other a break during the busy on-call days. On one such evening Riaad assessed an elderly man who had been brought in by his son. The man was unwell but Riaad didn't think that his condition warranted admission to the hospital, so he sent him home with medication. His son protested, insisting that his father be admitted, but Riaad stood his ground. The man died later that night at home. The following morning the son came in to inform Riaad, and he made it clear that he held him responsible.

"That really affected me. I wondered how differently things would have turned out had I made a different decision."

I suspect that many of us carry certain decisions with us, bringing them out every so often to subject them to what-ifs and if-onlys, only to tuck them away again when all the wondering has done nothing to alter the outcome.

"How did you find Site B?" I asked.

His brow furrowed. "Tough. I will never forget one Saturday morning on call," he began.

Immediately a familiar scene sprang to mind. I remembered how on Saturday mornings at Site B the emergency unit resembled a baby clinic, as mothers who worked during the week made use of this time to bring their children to the clinic; scores of them would wait on the benches outside the doctors' cubicles. Most of the time the children had mild respiratory tract infections, an ailment common in children and exacerbated by the paraffin stoves and poor ventilation in the township's informal dwellings. A short period on the nebuliser to open up their air passages and some medication to take home were usually all that was required. Their numbers would start to decrease by late afternoon, in time for the first casualties of the day's drinking sessions to start trickling in.

That day Riaad had been working non-stop since his shift had begun at eight o'clock. By four in the afternoon he realised that he hadn't eaten and he decided to take a break.

"I had just sat down to eat when there was a knock on the door of the tearoom. An ambulance had brought in a man with a dislocated shoulder and they wanted me to assess him."

"Was he in bad shape?"

"Well, no, that guy was fine; I was confident of being able to manage him at the clinic. The thing is, as I was going to the ambulance to sign him in, I was approached by another man who said that his son was very ill and he wanted me to come and see him. I asked that man to wait a bit while I went to the ambulance."

He paused, and again he looked into the distance. "By the time I got to see the boy he was blue. We tried to resuscitate him, but we couldn't."

He looked at me directly. "I'll never forget the look on that father's face as he held his dead son in his arms. I understand his anguish even more now that I have my own children."

I began to appreciate how the prospect of pursuing another path could have been alluring for him. I also wondered whether the comedy had been valuable in helping him to cope with the challenges of his job.

He responded by slipping into comedian mode, performing a brilliant impersonation of the nursing staff at Site B. "Why must we kill ourselves, Doctor? Why?"

I burst out laughing, partly out of enjoyment of the comedic act, but also because I recognised that don't-worry-it's-tea-time attitude that was so prevalent at Site B. Like me Riaad was frustrated by the lethargy and resignation that many of the staff displayed.

He continued. "I could understand the nurses who had been there for many years becoming disillusioned by the system, but I witnessed that attitude even in the new recruits. I wanted to shake them out of their lethargy and say to them: *You just got here; of course you must kill yourself!*"

I chuckled. One of the nurses I had worked with used to sit eating while I saw patients. Either that or she wandered around the clinic socialising.

"It's like we were thrown into a system that was in complete contrast to everything we were taught about focus, dedication and hard work," he added. I nodded in agreement.

"When did you know that medicine wasn't for you?" I asked.

"After community service I started doing locums and getting more involved in comedy. Opportunities opened up and I took them. You could say that I took the path of least resistance," he said with a wry smile.

Perhaps I was projecting my own feelings when I asked him if he felt any guilt about leaving. He pondered my question for a few seconds. "A little. I still love the profession, though I don't think I'll ever practise as a doctor again. But I'd like to contribute in some way, especially now that I have a bit of a public profile."

Riaad was being modest. He has achieved considerable success as a stand-up comedian, becoming something of a household name in the country. In 2012 he broke into acting, playing the lead role in the movie *Material,* for which he received the South African Film and Television Award for best actor. Also in that year his comedy show, *Keeping You in Stitches,* helped to raise funds for UCT's faculty of health sciences. The money was used to purchase a vehicle to transport medical students to the faculty's rural training site in Vredenburg on the Western Cape's west coast. This was Riaad's way of contributing to a profession he still loves.

Riaad's acting career received a major boost in 2013 when he played the role of the struggle icon Ahmed Kathrada in the epic biographical film, *Mandela: Long Walk to Freedom.*

"Do you have any regrets?" I asked.

"Regrets, I have a few," he crooned, and then he shook his head with a chuckle. "I can't live my life with regrets. There are things that I feel sad about, of course, but I prefer to focus on what's working in my life."

Isn't that what we all want? Lives that work.

13 | A Culture of Coping

The fact that so many of the doctors I interviewed were women wasn't lost on me. Perhaps it was mere coincidence, brought about as a result of my initial search through my own contacts and former colleagues. I began to actively seek out male doctors to interview, and though I did find a few, I did consider that this may point to a greater tendency for women to leave the medical profession.

While I fully acknowledge that my findings were purely anecdotal and that the small number of doctors interviewed rendered the findings unscientific, I nevertheless began to ask myself whether female doctors are more likely to walk away.

One doctor didn't mince her words when she pointed to the female doctors she had studied with who had left. "They are letting too many women into medical schools," Anthea* said.

She must have noticed me wince because she quickly added, "Don't get me wrong, I'm a complete feminist. I just think that at some point women will want to go off and start families. They want flexibility, so they are unlikely to want to be in the trenches dealing with gunshot wounds in casualty units and working after hours."

I couldn't help thinking how familiar this argument sounded. It had been used for years to keep women out of boardrooms and army barracks. Hadn't we fought and won this battle already?

Anthea graduated from UCT in 1998 and went off to Helen Joseph Hospital in Johannesburg for her internship, followed by a year as a response doctor in the ambulance service during her community service. Though she enjoyed emergency medicine as it appealed to her results-driven nature, it wasn't enough to keep her in the profession. She was frustrated by the inefficiency in the health system, and the sense that she was simply plugging a hole in the dyke.

"Most patients were disempowered and poor; they did not have the education or the resources to look after themselves, so by the time they came to hospital they had already reached the end of the line. What could medicine really do for them?"

After a few years spent in the United Kingdom Anthea elected to do an MBA before moving to financial services. Her ultimate goal is to work in the non-profit sector, focusing primarily on education. "This is where real change can be made," she said.

As I listened to Anthea I realised that what I had initially regarded as an outright sexist statement from her was probably just her pragmatic personality coming through. She came across as someone who didn't suffer fools – or an inefficient health system – lightly.

Ironically she reminded me of some of the female specialists who were my lecturers at medical school. "Severe" is the word that comes to mind to describe them, particularly the older ones. It sometimes felt that they were deliberately being harsh because that was the only way they knew to be in order to be taken seriously. In fairness to them, I can understand that strategy; in the period during which they qualified, I imagine it must have been difficult for women to graduate from medical schools, and even more so to rise through the ranks of the male-dominated profession.

When I graduated in 1999, life for an educated woman was much easier than it had been. Our choices were wide open; we could rise as far as we dared to aspire. It has always been my belief that being a woman in the workplace is merely a matter of biology, but I also appreciate that female doctors need to make gender-specific choices, much like their counterparts in other sectors. After all, many work environments are still not accommodating of the many demands placed on women's lives. It doesn't help that, in addition, medical practice is characterised by long hours and working in potentially dangerous environments.

Anthea's manner pointed to a factor that in my view was much more relevant than gender as an indicator of the type of people who become doctors. Typically the people who get into medicine are driven, ambitious, high achievers with perfectionist tendencies; the kind of people who believe that if you want something done properly you do it yourself.

I am certainly like that; I typify the so-called Type-A personality that marks doctors out. I have low tolerance for inefficiency and uncertainty, and I often struggle with change. I found it frustrating that in the real world, patients weren't as predictable as I would have liked and that medical problems didn't always have clear-cut solutions. Sometimes there were just too many questions where answers should have been.

In those early days when I was fresh out of medical school I thought that what I'd learned from my textbooks was the sum total of all that I needed to know about the human body, its failings and the accompanying treatments to restore it back to health. It came as a shock to me to realise that there were significant gaps in our knowledge, and that allopathic medicine wasn't the complete answer to health and wellbeing.

There were half-hearted attempts in our training to sensitise us to other treatment modalities, but the attitude of our lecturers left me in no doubt that they viewed the Western medical model as superior to all the others. It was not uncommon on a ward round for a senior doctor to dismiss incorrect dosages prescribed by an inexperienced doctor as "homeopathic" as they were unlikely to have a therapeutic effect.

I grew to expect that my training would provide me with answers, so I was stumped when the striving and probing sometimes amounted to naught.

During my internship in the UK, I had a patient who I grew quite close to. Clive was a good-natured man, a dream patient who never complained. He presented to the hospital with symptoms of deteriorating health and swollen extremities, and he was admitted to our medical team for further investigation. We searched tirelessly to find the cause of his complaints, brought in specialists in all the various fields from nephrologists to haematologists to hepatologists, but no one could get to the bottom of what was wrong with him.

At one point I even requested a full-body CT scan. I knew that this was bad medicine, a shotgun approach to a mystery that we couldn't solve. I walked the form to the radiologist personally to explain the situation because I knew it would have been returned rejected if I had submitted it through the usual channels.

We spent a significant portion of the NHS budget on Clive, to no avail. He simply drifted away and we couldn't bring him back.

His wife, Sarah, called me some weeks after Clive died to thank me for the effort that I had made. She had often been at his side, and I had grown to like them both. They had been accommodating, even when it meant that Clive would be subjected to further investigation by yet another team of specialist doctors.

Clive wasn't the only question mark that lingered from my days as a doctor. There were other mysteries along the way, patients whose diagnoses remained elusive despite our best attempts to find them.

In the years since leaving medicine I've learned that life doesn't always have clear answers, and even when it does we can't always understand them. Back then, though, I was too concerned with finding those answers, and regarded the inability to find them as failure on my part. I had not yet learned to let go. I wonder whether medical students today know that they aren't going to cure everybody or that they will sometimes not know what to do or how to do it.

A former classmate from medical school sent me this quote from *The Cost of Living*[5] by the Indian author and activist Arundhati Roy: "To love. To be loved. To never forget your own insignificance. To never get used to the unspeakable violence and the vulgar disparity of life around you . . . Above all, to watch. To try and understand. To never look away. And never, never to forget."

Noelle* pointed out to me how the quotation spoke to so much of what she had found challenging during her time as a doctor – the watching, trying to understand, never looking away. "I had to face the tension of disparity every day. The challenge has been something I have been grateful for but it was certainly something that I felt unprepared for," she said.

---

5 Roy, Arundhati. *The Cost of Living*. New York: Modern Library, 1999.

Noelle stopped practising medicine in 2010. By her own admission she had taken her work too seriously, and she had struggled to distance herself from the daily challenges of her job. She took it all personally, launched herself into challenges with zeal, only to find herself frustrated by bureaucratic bungles and organisational inefficiencies. She found herself hitting a brick wall while working in an HIV clinic that served a high-prevalence community in an informal settlement on Cape Town's False Bay coast. She was on a path that could only lead to disillusionment and burnout.

It took a lot for Noelle to accept that she wasn't going to save everybody or do as much for her patients as she knew was theoretically possible. After ten years of practice she left medicine and she now devotes her energy to raising her young children.

While she was still practising, it was only through mindfulness practice – the practice of focusing our attention on the here and now, without judgement or expectation – that Noelle was able to cope with the limitations of her job. She suggested that this type of intervention should be an integral part of medical training.

It seems to me that the very traits that enable doctors to undergo six rigorous years of study and to work under challenging conditions in the South African health care system are the very qualities that often work against them. When we push through difficulties without stopping to reflect or ask for help, we are putting our own wellbeing at risk.

Brené Brown, a renowned American scholar, author and public speaker, wrote in her book titled *The Gifts of Imperfection*[6]: "We can-

6 Brown, Brené. *The Gifts of Imperfection: Let Go of Who You Think You're Supposed to Be and Embrace Who You Are.* Center City, MN: Hazelden, 2010.

not selectively numb emotions; when we numb the painful emotions, we also numb the positive emotions."

I have to wonder how many of my former colleagues struggled to cope with the demands of the profession and the trying conditions under which we worked. I went looking for answers at Valkenberg Hospital in Observatory, the oldest dedicated psychiatric hospital in the Western Cape. Valkenberg provides specialist psychiatric services for the province and is a training facility for psychiatrists and psychiatric nurses. The hospital was established in 1891 to accommodate mentally ill patients, many of whom had been virtually banished – along with lepers and other chronically ill patients – to the Robben Island Lunatic Asylum.

I arrived at Valkenberg on a cool, damp morning. I was surprised not to see any patients about as I made my way to the Education Centre. When I did my psychiatry rotation there during fifth year I would regularly spot patients milling about on the open grounds. Perhaps the weather had kept them indoors.

I smiled at the honesty of the hospital's motto etched on a plaque in the foyer of the Education Centre: *Sometimes to Cure, Often to Relieve, Always to Comfort*. As I waited for my meeting, I looked around at the place I'd last seen nearly fifteen years before, and memories came flooding back. Psychiatry was one of the subjects that many students didn't seem to take seriously. We would sometimes joke that only mad doctors went on to become psychiatrists. Some of our lecturers did little to discourage this sentiment.

During one particularly memorable lecture, the psychiatrist attempted to illustrate the symptoms of a panic attack by recounting his own experience. He was animated as he spoke about the intense feeling of dread that overcame him as he walked to his car at a busy shopping mall. His heart pounded, he broke out in a sweat, and he was certain he was about to die. As he spoke the students exchanged looks that seemed to say: *So it's true what they say about psychiatrists.*

I was met by Dr Harrison*, a specialist psychiatrist who had worked at Valkenberg for over twenty years. Dr Harrison had taught me as a student, and I remembered him being thoughtful and intense. I glanced over at him as he ushered me to his office; save for the streaks of grey in his blond hair, he looked exactly the same as I remembered.

I started off clumsily as I tried to articulate why I had come to see him. It all came out in a heap – the conversations with other ex-medics, my own disillusionment, my suspicion that this emotional and psychological distress was more widespread than a handful of disenchanted doctors. I wanted to understand the extent of the problem; more than that I wanted to know what kind of help was available for doctors in distress.

When he spoke his responses were measured, like someone who knows how closely the words we utter reflect the thoughts we think.

"We are not doing well at looking after ourselves and each other," he began. "Many people in this profession feel exhausted and overwhelmed, yet very few seek help."

"Why do you think that is?" I asked.

He paused for a moment. "There is enormous pressure about being seen to cope. People don't want to let themselves down, or to let others down."

I wanted to know what his experience was with doctors and students in distress. He told me about a multidisciplinary committee, based at UCT Medical School, which is meant to serve as a mechanism for identifying and assisting students who are experiencing emotional and psychological distress. "There have been a number of students over the years who have experienced difficulties. As you know, the pressure is enormous; some students simply crack under it," he said.

"What about doctors who are struggling?" I asked.

He shook his head. "There is very little support, and what there is is inadequate and disorganised. Some will seek help from colleagues in the private sector, and others . . ." His voice trailed off and I waited for him to continue. "There is an unacknowledged proportion who will self-medicate with substances, benzodiazepines or antidepressants. It's tragic that drugs are used as a coping mechanism."

I probed further. "Where does this all come from? How is it allowed to get to that point?"

Even as I asked the questions I knew what the answers would be. The culture of coping and resilience is deeply entrenched in the medical profession. It starts early on in our training – the hours, the workload, the exposure to gruesome pathology and trauma. Dr Harrison referred to them as "rituals of induction and brutalisation". These can be overwhelming, and shutting down and pushing through is often the most expedient way to cope.

"We don't reflect on our experiences. There is fear that introspection might lead to questions which we are often too scared to ask ourselves. Have I wasted all this time? Was I foolish to do this? Am I naïve and idealistic, a hopeless romantic? Can I do anything else? Instead we create this illusion of coping when in fact we are shutting down the critical faculties of questioning and reflection."

I saw it in those fifth-year students at Salt River Mortuary; that bravado, the façade that says: *I'm not bothered by the fact that there's a dead person in front of me*. During my time at medical school we would glamorise the more gruelling aspects of the job. There was a special badge of honour for those people who worked the longest hours and saw the most challenging cases. We wanted it to be difficult and harsh; we wanted to earn our stripes in that way, never once stopping to ask what we were doing to ourselves in the process.

Dr Harrison continued. "We are supposed to be helping other people in distress, yet we can't look after ourselves. What does that say about our competence, capacity and effectiveness?"

"So what is the solution?" I asked.

"We need to be honest about what's going on."

He made his point by telling me of an incident the previous day when one of the psychiatry registrars was assaulted by a patient. When Dr Harrison called the registrar into his office to find out how he was doing, his response was: "I'm fine, I'm coping."

"It's ludicrous, of course, that he would be coping. It was a very traumatic event, yet he couldn't say that he was afraid or anxious. In the twenty years that I've practised as a psychiatrist only one colleague has ever said to me that they were not coping."

He paused briefly and shrugged. "I understand the registrar's reluctance to speak up, though. We work in a hierarchical environment. How do you admit to your supervisor that you are traumatised?"

"Is it worse for junior doctors?" I asked.

He shook his head. "It goes right through the ranks. I think if we knew the number of doctors who either drop out or struggle on miserably we would be shocked. It's a poor reflection on the profession."

But how do you admit that you are struggling when there's work to be done? When I worked at Jooste we were informed about a counselling service, which was available if we needed it, but I never thought to use it. Taking time out to go and speak to a counsellor would have meant burdening my colleagues with an even greater workload. I pushed on, until I felt that the only way I could mend myself was to leave.

I was also reminded of my classmate Thandi*. Would it have made any difference if she had left medicine sooner? Thandi and I studied together but we didn't know each other well. We had some mutual friends and we would sometimes bump into each other at social gatherings and exchange polite small talk. She was pretty and jolly, with cheeks that dimpled when she smiled and a ready giggle tucked at the end of each sentence. She attracted a considerable amount of male attention.

The rumours started circulating in our fifth year. Thandi was recovering from the sudden break-up of a brief but passionate romance, and we had initially assumed that she was mourning the loss of the relationship when she took to keeping to herself. But after a while her friends began to notice a change in her behaviour and it made them worry. She became secretive and paranoid, believing that her ex-boyfriend was stalking her. At first her friends believed her, but they realised something was wrong when her paranoia became extreme and took on a delusional quality.

She was admitted to C23, the psychiatric emergency and assessment unit at Groote Schuur Hospital, for treatment. She continued outpatient treatment when she was discharged, and we all thought she was out of the woods when she passed her final-year exams and qualified as a doctor.

Thandi suffered a relapse when she began to practise. She moved to Pretoria and her friends didn't know what was going on with her. She became extremely secretive, reporting that she was concerned that people were after her. The details of her life became sketchy – she would stay out of communication with her friends for extended periods of time. She took to sleeping in hotels to evade her alleged tormentors, and she refused to drive her own car or use her own cellphone as she believed that these had been fitted with tracking devices.

Thandi's life spiralled out of control and in 2008 she committed suicide with a cocktail of over-the-counter drugs. Hers wasn't an isolated case of psychiatric illness among my former classmates. Another committed suicide in 2012, and during the course of our studies a handful of students took leaves of absence and underwent treatment for psychiatric conditions.

To what extent did their chosen profession exacerbate their impairment? Would their illnesses have surfaced irrespective of their work? I cannot speculate on the answers to these questions. What I do know is that being in that environment placed too great a strain on my own mental wellbeing.

14 | Own Goal

When I began writing this book I was conscious of wanting it to be an introspective examination of the reasons that led me to abandon my medical career. I wanted to take responsibility for my actions and decisions without laying the blame elsewhere. It is undeniable, however, that the system under which I worked played an important role in my decision, and I believe it is a major contributor to the exodus of doctors from the South African public health sector.

It is a broken system in general, and in some cases it has collapsed entirely. For one doctor it was this brokenness and the apparent inability and unwillingness of its leaders to bring about change that drove him to seek opportunities in the private sector.

Ludwe* is an avid sports enthusiast and he began our conversation over coffee by using an analogy from his favourite sport.

"Manchester United recently announced that Sir Alex Ferguson would retire as team manager after 26 years at the helm. Over that period, Sir Alex built Man U into a very successful club. Sure they dipped from time to time, but overall they did very well. Now compare that with our own Chippa United where we went through at least four coaches in one season. Is it any wonder that the team was relegated after only a brief stint in the Premier Soccer League?"

"Is that what's wrong with our health system, then? Chopping and changing?" I asked.

"It is," he said. "That's what's going on in the health sector. MECs, director-generals and hospital managers change all the time; people are appointed for political reasons, and there is little by way of consistency in leadership. And we have the results that reflect that."

Ludwe is no stranger to the world of politics. He was born and raised in the former Transkei and when he completed his schooling in 1994, he was awarded a bursary by the government to study at the University of KwaZulu-Natal. In his first year he was recruited into the political structures on campus.

He laughed as he recalled his bafflement during the early political meetings. "These guys were speaking English but I had no idea what they were saying. It was *inter alia* . . . *whereby* . . . *vis-à-vis*. . . I had to learn the lingo." He picked it up quickly and he rose to the leadership structures of the Student Representative Council on the medical campus until his graduation in 2001.

I could see Ludwe as a leader. He was charming and good looking, and he had a way about him that I could see would draw people to him. He used these traits in his favour when he began his internship at Cecilia Makiwane Hospital in the township of Mdantsane in the Eastern Cape. "I would sit and eat lunch with the nurses. It was unusual for a doctor to do that, but for me it felt natural. I was a young and inexperienced doctor, and I respected their knowledge and experience. As a result I learned a lot from those nurses," he said.

Ludwe devoted himself to his work at the hospital. As enthusiastically as he forged relationships with the nurses he also became involved in the doctor's committee and the Junior Doctors' Association of South Africa (JUDASA). And he took a keen interest in his patients' lives. "I got to know many of my patients' families. They would call me with updates on their relatives' health, and insist to be seen by me when they came to the hospital. It was great, but also very tough. HIV was killing people in numbers and I saw the devastation it was causing to these families. It became very demoralising."

Ludwe stayed at Cecilia Makiwane for his community service and the year after as a medical officer. But the piecemeal difference he was making in patients' lives was getting to him. He felt he could have more of an impact within a leadership position and he applied for and was offered a position as a medical superintendent at Frontier Hospital in Queenstown.

After a few months in Queenstown he realised he was floundering. "When you study medicine you learn nothing else except how to treat patients. I had no managerial skills, and I really felt it." He registered for a modular MBA at Stellenbosch University but he struggled to make sense of the new concepts while keeping up his work at the hospital. He was forced to abandon his studies in 2006.

Then an inspiring opportunity was offered to him. Ludwe was asked to be part of a specialist team tasked with turning around the Eastern Cape's health system. He jumped at the opportunity; this was the chance, which he had craved, to make a difference. But his enthusiasm was short lived when the initiative became mired in politics. Inertia set in and other members of the team started leaving. Ludwe stayed until it was just him and the project co-ordinator left. He was then forced to concede that he was wasting his time.

"The failure of this project reinforced the idea that specialised managerial skills were needed in order to get the job done. People didn't know how to deliver; it was endemic in the system."

He negotiated with hospital management to get funding for a full-time MBA, and he relocated his young family to Cape Town. This time the results reflected his dedicated focus and he completed his MBA in 2008.

Ludwe went back to the Eastern Cape in 2010, but the management team he had previously worked with had been replaced and conflict arose between him and the new leaders. He elected to return to Cecilia Makiwane to work as a casualty officer.

"Did this not feel like a demotion?" I asked.

"That's what everyone said, even the nurses who I'd worked so well with in the past. They were pleased to have me back, but they could see that I didn't belong there any more."

"How did you feel about being there?"

"It felt hopeless. There was a culture of disservice and apathy, and it went right through the entire structure of the hospital, from the hospital management, the professional staff and even the support personnel. I finally had to accept that I was not making a difference in that environment, so I started making plans to leave," he said. He left medical practice in October 2010 to join a national medical aid scheme.

"Was it the right move to go to the private sector?" I asked him.

He shrugged. "The challenges in the private sector are different. I see an incredible amount of waste, whereas in government hospitals you try to stretch limited resources as far as possible. In the private sector you pour money into patients until their very last breath."

I could see that the Ludwe who wanted to make a difference

hadn't died along with his medical career, and I wondered whether he had regrets about leaving. He snapped back in his characteristic style: "Not at all. I know that I wasn't meant to spend my life putting my finger in dark orifices. Other people can do that, not me," he sniggered.

He paused then grew serious again. "But I still want to make a difference. I think we all have that duty, whether as doctors, lawyers, bus drivers . . . whatever."

"How is that difference going to be made in the health sector if so many of us are leaving?"

He looked at me squarely. "Leadership is key. There has got to be the will to do things differently, and the courage to do what is needed. There is too much focus on politics and not enough on delivery."

My conversation with Ludwe rang in my ears when I read a sobering report in September 2013 indicating that the shambles in the management of the Eastern Cape's health system went even deeper than Ludwe had suggested. The report, titled "Death and Dying in the Eastern Cape", was compiled jointly by the health advocacy group the Treatment Action Campaign, and the public interest law centre, SECTION27. It described how the system of health care in the province had deteriorated to the point of collapse.

In many areas facilities were crumbling; there was a lack of medication and equipment, non-existent emergency services and critical shortages of personnel. The writers lay much of the responsibility for this collapse at the door of the officials tasked with managing the provincial health system and the politicians charged with its oversight.

Ludwe had seen all this coming. He had recognised the need to supplement his clinical expertise with managerial training, and after completing his MBA he had gone back with the intention to contribute, only to find that the powers that be saw no use for his skills. Instead over the years the health system was allowed to crumble while those with the power to stop the rot were lining their own pockets, leaving patients to fend for themselves.

I can't imagine what it must be like for the doctors who work in this kind of environment. It must take a special kind of individual to choose to be there; I know a number of my former classmates are doing sterling work at Zithulele Hospital in the impoverished Oliver Tambo District Municipality (which includes the city of Mthatha). I can only admire their fortitude and commitment. Being a doctor is tough enough without working within a system that is falling apart at the seams.

It will be interesting to see whether the pronouncements made by the minister of health in the aftermath of the report's release, in which he committed to the development of a plan to address the crisis, will be followed through with decisive action. I am inclined towards optimism with the current minister. As Mark Sonderup put it: "At least now we have a health minister who acknowledges the scale of the challenge that exists and is prepared to do something about it. Those years of denial set this country back decades and now we have a lot of catching up to do."

Concerted efforts have been made in recent years to address the country's health challenges and the resulting health gains are encouraging. However one particular intervention to bolster the number of doctors in the public health system remains baffling – the training of South African medical students in Cuba.

In its quest to alleviate the critical shortage of doctors in the country, the South African government entered into an agreement with its counterparts in Cuba in the 1990s. Initially this agreement saw Cuban doctors practising in South Africa, particularly in rural hospitals. The programme later evolved to include the training of local doctors in Cuba.

Students are recruited into the programme on the basis of academic merit as well as their disadvantaged backgrounds and rural origins. These students are then flown to Cuba where Spanish is the primary language of instruction. They spend the first year learning the language, and thereafter they undergo training at the medical schools, learning the Cuban model, which emphasises primary health care and community medicine. It is a recognised fact that Cuba has some of the best health indicators in the world.

Though the primary care approach is commendable, as this is where the greatest need lies in South Africa, the disease profile in Cuba is quite markedly unlike that of South Africa. Most notable is the fact that Cuba has some of the lowest HIV rates in the world, whereas South Africa has the highest. One can't help but wonder what these students are being trained for.

Upon completion of their studies the students enter the medical training system back home, joining the final-year students at the country's medical schools. Needless to say, often they struggle. They need to relearn much what they have already covered in Cuba, only this time in English. They also need to familiarise themselves with the diseases that are most prevalent in the South African setting.

At the beginning of 2013 the Cuban training programme was thrown into the spotlight when a number of students went on strike in protest over their stipends and meals. The government dismissed their claims, and I initially failed to understand their grievance given that their studies, accommodation, food and stipends were being fully paid for by the two governments. On closer inspection, though, I have to wonder whether this ultimately futile protest action was a symptom of a more fundamental challenge. After all, these are students from impoverished backgrounds who had likely never travelled outside their own country. Then they have been thrust into a foreign environment, away from their families, and with another language and culture to adjust to. I imagine the combination of culture shock and homesickness – in addition to the pressures of their medical studies – must be a lot for them to deal with.

While I understand that the shortages of doctors cannot be allowed to continue in a country that so desperately needs them, I fail to see the merits of this programme. I struggled with the realities of practising medicine in South Africa, but having been trained here at least I knew to expect them. What then for these students?

15 | Point of Change

Chris Hani Baragwanath Hospital was a prominent landmark of my childhood. I imagine the hospital – known locally as Bara – occupies a similar place in the minds of many Sowetans. The iconic hospital, the largest on the African continent, is situated at the entrance of the sprawling township, and it is in many ways a microcosm of the broader population that it serves.

As a child I saw the hospital every day as I commuted between my home and the city, and over the years I witnessed its gradual transformation. In my earliest memories Bara was a towering monolith opposite Soweto's major transport interchange, its perimeter fence strewn with plastic bags. At Christmas time migrant workers would gather outside the hospital, their luggage overflowing as they waited for the buses and taxis that would take them back to their rural homes for the holidays. Gradually a wall was built on which graffiti artists practised their craft, and later the graffiti made way for health promotion murals. In recent years the main entrance on Old Potchefstroom Road has been transformed into an ornate structure befitting a facility of this stature.

I remember the grounds of the hospital as a maze of buildings. I had been there on a number of occasions as a child to visit family members, and it seemed that every time I went there it would take an inordinate length of time for us to find where we were meant to be. There were the numerous visits to see my father when he was hospitalised after particularly serious epileptic seizures; there were also visits to see aunts and uncles. The last time I was there was in 2001. My grandmother had suffered a massive stroke, which had left her partially paralysed and had affected her speech and cognitive function. I'd qualified as a doctor then and as I'd stood around the bed with my extended family I had looked around and felt strongly that this sprawling hospital was the last place I would want to work.

Outside of my personal associations with the hospital I knew of its reputation as a place of high drama. Even as thrill-seeking medical students we had a sense that practising at Bara was not for the faint hearted. In recent years my only connection with the hospital was through the newspaper headlines that cropped up from time to time, most of them negative. "Baragwanath Hospital Battling to Cope", "Baragwanath Doctors Not Paid Overtime", "Two-year Waiting List for Operations".

This was the place where a young doctor was posted in her internship year. It was a year that proved instrumental in the shaping of her expectations about her career.

I met with Roxy* at a coffee shop near her home in Tokai in June 2013. I noticed in her manner that she was different from most of the other doctors I'd met with. She was soft spoken and reserved, and she exuded an air of someone who was at peace with where she was. I asked whether my assessment of her mental state was accurate.

She smiled. "Yes, I'm very happy in medicine," she said. She giggled and added, "I'm a little nervous at the moment, though."

"Why is that?"

"I start a new job tomorrow," she said. Roxy was due to start work as a sessional doctor in the oncology unit at Groote Schuur. She would be working with adults after a number of years in paediatrics, and she was understandably anxious about how she would make the adjustment. One thing she was certain of, however, was her place in the medical profession.

Roxy was a relative latecomer to medicine. After finishing school in 1990 she enrolled for a Bachelor of Commerce degree at Wits. "I didn't really know what I wanted to do with my life," she said.

This seemed unusual. "Didn't you always want to be a doctor?" I asked.

"Not at all," she said.

After graduating she spent five years in the commercial environment before feeling that she needed to find something that was more fulfilling. She was surprised when the results of an aptitude test suggested she pursue a medical career, but she warmed to the idea and applied to Wits Medical School where she studied until 2005.

When she began her internship she was idealistic about what her medical training would enable her to do. But the year at Bara was to be the undoing of the ideal she'd gone in there with.

"It was a completely unhealthy year," she said.

Roxy rotated through the paediatrics, trauma and internal medicine disciplines during that year, and her time in the trauma unit was especially sobering.

"I worked with another intern looking after a six-bed resuscitation unit with little supervision from the senior doctors. The things that we saw and did were just insane."

"How did you cope?"

She shook her head. "I didn't. There were some mornings after a night on call when I would stop off for a glass of wine on my way home. It was just crazy."

This was the Bara whose reputation had lived in my mind. The trauma unit in particular was said to be one of the busiest in the world.

The craziness of her internship prompted her to seek a more peaceful posting in her community service year, and she chose a regional hospital in KwaZulu-Natal, not far from the Umfolozi Game Reserve. Though she described one of the senior doctors there as "negligent, useless and dangerous", she had more support as the hospital had a large complement of foreign doctors. It was the respite she needed to reconnect with her passion and commitment to her job, and she learned a lot during that year. More importantly, she felt that her work was having a positive impact. At Bara she had felt that she was simply doing her best to keep her head above water in a situation in which she felt out of her depth.

When she completed her community service she went back to Bara where she worked in paediatric HIV. Her future plans were to specialise in oncology and palliative care.

Roxy had no desire to leave medicine. She attributed her continued love for the profession to the more realistic approach which she had adopted. "My expectations have changed over the years. I am more realistic about what I can achieve and I no longer give myself such a hard time."

Roxy looked genuinely content with where her career had taken her, and she had made sense of the rocky start to her job. She has a young daughter and she has structured her work to accommodate her responsibilities as a mother. She will have no night-time calls when she begins the sessional work, although this will change when she is a registrar. I have no doubt that she will deal with it with the same level-headedness that was so plainly evident during our conversation.

Roxy displayed the kind of maturity that I didn't have at the time that I was practising. Sure, she'd had a horrific internship, but she'd got over it. Perhaps it also helped that she went into medicine as an older student, with few expectations and none of the romantic ideals that I had going in. She took each day as it came, and when it was over she moved on.

I took it personally, and I found it difficult to move on. I was too angry to look beyond the drudgery of my day, disappointed that my dream job was messy and frustrating, and I guess I was also too stubborn to be flexible. When I looked ahead all I could see was more of the same, and there was no way I was prepared to put myself through that. I see now that I was too immersed in it; perhaps all I needed was a change in perspective.

Such a shift in perspective is exactly what has kept another doctor's love for medicine alive. Francois Bonnici was born to be a doctor. Both his parents are respected physicians in Cape Town, and he grew up with medicine as an integral part of his family life. As youngsters Francois and his sister would often join the children's camps organised by the Red Cross Children's Hospital, and it was not uncommon for them to spend Christmas at Red Cross when their parents were working. Immersed as he was in the profession from a young age, when the time came for him to choose a career, medicine was the natural choice.

Francois' upbringing influenced his decision to enter the medical profession in another way too. His family had always been deeply entrenched in the teachings of St Francis of Assisi and the Franciscan philosophy of social justice and service to the poor. By becoming a doctor Francois would have the opportunity to continue this work.

I didn't know Francois personally when I was at medical school, but I knew of him. He was a year my senior, and he had a formidable reputation as a brilliant student. Whenever I spotted him in the hospital he seemed to be bursting with energy, like someone with things to do and places to get to. I remember that he had unusually long hair back then, which would fall into his face as he walked in his characteristic way. Why would someone so talented, and so entrenched in the medical profession through family ties, choose to walk away?

When Francois began his medical studies he immersed himself in the science of medicine and he excelled academically. It was when the clinical training began in fourth year, however, that he realised that the human element was missing in what he was being taught. He sought to remedy the situation; he wanted to learn how to interact with patients and to deal with the difficult issues, so he enrolled on a counselling course and worked as a Lifeline counsellor during his final two years at medical school.

Francois graduated top of his class in 1998 and he went on to work in Windhoek in Namibia for his internship year. At the time Namibia didn't have a medical school, so Francois was sent there with over a dozen other interns as part of South Africa's co-operation agreement with its neighbouring country. Armed with his first-class qualification and the desire to change the world, Francois went there expecting that he would make a positive impact.

The new graduates were confronted with a challenge they hadn't expected. Inexperienced though they were, they ended up effectively running the country's tertiary hospital, with little supervision from senior doctors. What little support they had was erratic and at times clinically unreliable. They floundered in the face of the challenge.

In addition to the usual demands of tertiary-level medicine, they had to deal with an explosion in the country of the incidence of HIV infection, which they could do little about without the necessary antiretroviral therapy. In addition the Congo War was raging, and military trucks and helicopters regularly brought casualties to the hospital.

The year proved to be a traumatic induction for the idealistic young doctor. By the end of his internship Francois realised that he had faced 44 resuscitations during the year, only one of which was successful – a child, who died three days later. Something clearly wasn't working, and he undertook to uncover the cause of the breakdown and to find solutions.

Francois took up a scholarship at Oxford University after the year in Namibia. He had initially intended to pursue a high-level academic degree in paediatrics, but after his experiences in Windhoek he elected to do a Masters in Public Health (MPH) instead.

The public health training provided him with the tools to implement new strategies and he returned to Namibia to initiate a programme in newborn care. During his internship he had been sensitised to the fact that the newborn period held a unique set of challenges and that mortality in this first month of life was under-recognised as a contributor to infant mortality as a whole. With his MPH, Francois was able set up initiatives to address this critical early stage of life specifically. Within four months of initiating the programme Francois's team had trained 450 nurses, opened twelve newborn care units and written the national policy on newborn care. This was a significant achievement, not only for newborn care in Namibia but also for what it taught Francois about overcoming challenges – that if a point of change could be found, then solutions could be implemented.

Francois returned to South Africa for his community service. Not one to follow convention, he negotiated with the Department of Health to work with them on newborn care programmes, using many of the strategies that had proved successful in Namibia. He felt his considerable experience would be wasted if he spent the year in a typical community service post. The Department agreed; he was based at Mowbray Maternity Hospital and his work covered 26 small hospitals throughout the Western Cape.

Francois later went back to Oxford where he completed an MBA, focusing particularly on social entrepreneurship and innovation. His love for clinical medicine lingered, though, even when he went on to occupy high-level positions working for international multilateral organisations around public-private partnerships in health. He yearned to be back in the wards, interacting with patients and making a difference at the coalface of medicine. He craved the joy he experienced when working with people, though he also recognised that this was where much of the heartache lay.

He made numerous attempts to get back into clinical practice. He took up registrar positions in paediatrics three times, and each time he abandoned his studies. As much as he loved working with patients, he realised that the system of health care didn't work. Why was it that the same child kept coming into hospital with diarrhoea? Why were preventable diseases not being prevented? It was the pursuit of the answers to these and other systemic challenges that drove Francois to look outside of the medical profession.

Francois was instrumental in the establishment of an institutional hub, based at UCT's Graduate School of Business, to research and initiate social innovation strategies and to train future leaders in this sphere. Their work has expanded beyond health to include education and poverty alleviation, as these sectors are interconnected. A notable focus of their work is to empower the people at the centre of the challenges to be part of the solution; his experience working with kangaroo mother care in Namibia had shown how innovative solutions needn't be high-tech in order to be effective. It is Francois' belief that the resources to bring about change are available in this country; they simply need to be harnessed and combined with creative thinking in order to bring about the desired results.

His formative medical training has been an invaluable foundation for the work he is now undertaking. He took to heart the wise words of his one-time mentor Dr Mamphela Ramphele – herself a medical doctor and more recently an academic, businesswoman and politician – when she told him that medicine was the training ground for empathetic leadership.

I was blown away by Francois' story and filled with admiration for the work he was doing. I have a number of friends who went into the public health arena and I am often struck by the far-reaching impact of their work. Listening to Francois, I wondered whether I could have done more. The challenges I faced were great, but they were not insurmountable. What if I'd tried harder to look for solutions? Or sought to impact the health system from a different angle as he had done? I needn't have kept hitting my head against the same hard wall. Would a change in perspective have helped to keep me in the profession?

16 | Against All Odds

Vicky* and I were at medical school together. During the early pre-clinical years we were in the same groups for some of the subjects. We had always got along; she was easy-going and friendly, the kind of person who chatted easily and got on well with others. Once the clinical training began in fourth year, however, we saw less of each other. We were often posted at different hospitals and we naturally drifted away from each other. We had no contact after our graduation in 1999.

I was pleasantly surprised then when Vicky rushed up to me at Kirstenbosch Botanical Gardens in May 2013. We embraced warmly and exchanged news on our lives since we'd last seen each other. She invited me to visit her at her place of work at one of the secondary-level public hospitals in Cape Town, and I gladly accepted.

When I arrived at the hospital two weeks later I wasn't sure what to expect. This was the public sector, after all. Would she have the time to talk to me? Might I need to go into theatre with her if she was called to an emergency?

I felt familiar pangs as I walked into the hospital. It was an old building, and though it was very clean, its walls could have done with a lick of paint. I asked where the operating theatre was and the security guard at the entrance pointed me down the corridor. I wondered who he thought I was and why I was there; he didn't ask what my business was going to theatre.

I made my way tentatively down the corridor, scanning each door for a sign of my destination. A patient stopped me along the way and I was about to tell her that I didn't work there when I recognised her – she was one of the floor staff at my local Woolworths Food store, and she had only stopped me to say hello. When we parted ways after a brief chat I laughed at myself for being so paranoid.

Vicky came to meet me outside the theatre and led me upstairs to the staff tearoom where she was finishing off a tutorial with a group of medical officers. I sat in on the final minutes of the tutorial and I marvelled at how far she'd come. Vicky was now a specialist anaesthetist and the head of the department of anaesthetics. It seemed just the other day that we had sat together in a tutorial at medical school half listening to a lecturer at the front of the room. How differently our careers had turned out.

Vicky's introduction to being a doctor was no different to all the other experiences I'd heard about, and was characterised by poor supervision, huge responsibility and the lack of adequate resources. When she told me about her community service posting, though, it seemed ludicrous, even by the generally poor standards.

She was assigned to Ekhombe Hospital in KwaZulu-Natal. It was the fifth choice on her community service application form; not only did she have little interest in going there, she didn't know much about it. But she was unmarried and childless so she was fair game for a posting in a far-flung location. She was given a map and background information on the hospital, most of which turned out to be inaccurate.

"We were told that it was a 150-bed hospital with two community service doctors, six medical officers, clinics nearby, and that doctors' accommodation was provided," she said.

The reality was very different. To get to the hospital she and another community service doctor had to drive to Nkandla in the heart of rural KwaZulu-Natal, where they were collected by a 4x4 vehicle to take them the rest of the 80 kilometres to the hospital. The facility itself was brand new and fully equipped – there was a fully fitted theatre, X-ray department and laboratory. But with no lab technicians, radiographer or theatre staff, all the shining new equipment was gathering dust.

"And the staff complement you were promised?" I asked.

She shook her head. "The six MOs turned out to be two Cuban doctors, one of whom was leaving. There were 100 beds and 300 inpatients, and when my colleague and I arrived the nurses ran out to greet us like we had come to save the day."

"You must have realised then that you were in for quite a challenge," I said.

She sniggered. "No. It was the so-called accommodation that brought the reality home to me. We were allocated a caravan next to the TB ward which we were supposed to call home."

We laughed at the absurdity of the situation, though Vicky admitted that at the time she was terrified. Her colleague burst into tears when she realised what they were in for.

"How did it go?" I asked.

She shook her head. "It didn't. I realised that it was just silly being there when I wasn't going to be helping. I turned the post down and asked to be posted elsewhere."

Vicky went on to work at Newcastle Provincial Hospital. "The first question they asked when I arrived was whether I had done anaesthetics. When I said I'd had a two-month rotation during my internship they were delighted. I instantly became the resident anaesthetist."

She spoke about her experiences casually, her characteristic good nature shining through. I remarked on her composure. "You seem to have taken it all in your stride," I said.

She shrugged. "It was tough, I'll tell you that. Remember that this was a dark period for all of us, people were dying all the time. I spent a big chunk of my community service year doing the death round in the mornings."

Even with her easy-going personality Vicky found the work challenging and she yearned for a different experience. She decided to go overseas after her community service, a decision largely motivated by a desire to gain experience working in a relatively normal environment. She worked in the UK's National Health Service and though the conditions were far better than what she'd experienced at home she also saw the perils of throwing money at health care.

She recounted the case of a heroin addict in the dialysis unit in which she had worked. His kidneys were shot from years of drug abuse. He was admitted onto the dialysis programme so that the machines would do the work that his kidneys were no longer able to perform.

"On the first day I met him he challenged me, demanding that I give him pethidine before he would submit to dialysis. I refused," she said.

"What did he say to that?" I asked.

"He told me he wouldn't dialyse, so I pointed out to him that he would die if he didn't. He stood his ground, probably thinking that he could intimidate me with the prospect of his death. But I wasn't fazed. I told him straight: 'If you were in my country, my friend, you wouldn't even be on this programme.' He must have realised that I wasn't budging and he gave in. Three days later he died at home from a drug overdose."

What this incident taught Vicky was the importance of balancing the use of resources with sound clinical judgement. "One of the upsides of having limited resources is that you are forced to think and make sensible decisions instead of just throwing money at problems. Huge amounts of resources are wasted when people don't have to say no. We see that happening in the private sector in this country," she said.

I watched Vicky as she continued talking. I couldn't help thinking that it was this pragmatic approach and her ability to see the upside of trying situations that had enabled her to continue working in the public sector. There was something else that I saw in her: she looked relaxed and at ease in her environment. I remarked on this and she laughed. "I'm the queen of my castle," she said.

She offered to take me on a tour of her domain, and I accepted, though I was concerned that we wouldn't have much time left to talk. We had already been together for close to an hour. "Don't you need to be in theatre soon?" I asked her.

"No, there's no theatre slate today," she said.

"Wow, nice job. Maybe I shouldn't have left after all," I joked.

She laughed. "It's not always like this. The nurses are on training for the day."

We walked out the tearoom and made our way downstairs to the various departments. She talked me through the work that they did at the hospital, in particular the work she had done in the four years she had been there as a specialist and the head of department.

When she arrived as a newly qualified specialist everything about her job was new, including the position itself. Previously the anaesthetics unit was run by two medical officers who were supported by sessional and locum doctors. Vicky's first task was to establish a fully fledged department.

"It was terrifying," she confessed. "The equipment was adequate but not world class; the ICU was in need of an overhaul and some of the staff had been in the same job for years without much upgrade to their skills. I spent a lot of time building relationships and buying equipment in those first few months." She chuckled. "In many ways the procurement issues were much easier to deal with than the relationships."

"Did you feel competent to do what you were doing?"

She raised her eyebrows. "No ways. I felt overwhelmed a lot of the time. I started to really look forward to being rostered for theatre because there I knew what I was doing. Plus, being stuck in theatre meant that I couldn't be called to meetings and I didn't have to manage anyone except the patient."

Vicky made impressive strides, and she owed much of her success to the support and guidance she received from the hospital's CEO.

"I have an excellent CEO. He helped me with the HR management issues, and he would gladly listen and offer guidance when I went to him to say that I felt out of my depth. He knows the policies and procedures and he showed me how to work with what we had to get the kinds of results we wanted. For the first time we didn't have to rely on Groote Schuur to make decisions for us."

"Have you achieved what you set to?"

She nodded. "When I first came here I had a vision for what I wanted to create. For me this place is like a family business. The children in the family will often go out to find their own way in the world, but ultimately they will return. I was initially here as an MO and I knew I'd be back. When I arrived as a consultant I took a long-term view, and each year we review where we're at and decide what adjustments need to be made."

I was impressed that Vicky had found her feet as a manager. "What about matters on the clinical front?" I asked.

"A lot was expected of me as a consultant and I had to deliver. For the first time I couldn't refer challenging cases to Groote Schuur for specialist opinion because I was it."

This too became a challenge that Vicky transformed to her advantage. The resources that are available in a teaching hospital like Groote Schuur – both in terms of equipment and personnel – are different to what is available at secondary-level facilities. Vicky learned to make decisions that were appropriate for her particular setting, with good results.

We interrupted our conversation when we arrived at the emergency room. Vicky exchanged greetings with one of the doctors on duty, and I looked around at the once familiar scene: patients on stretchers, machines bleeping, nurses adjusting drips and applying dressings. It felt like a lifetime ago that this was part of my daily experience.

When we moved on to the adjacent admissions ward Vicky showed me all the places where extra beds had been put in to make maximum use of the small space. "We make a plan where one needs to be made," she said.

When we got back to the tearoom we were joined by another former classmate. Jane* was now a paediatrician, and like Vicky she was in her element at this hospital. She was another member of the flock who had returned to see to the success of the family business. We spent some time looking through our medical school yearbook and reminiscing about our time at university before Jane left to rejoin her outpatients clinic.

I wondered whether Vicky's job had got her down at any point.

"I did think about leaving on a number of occasions, especially when I was a registrar at Groote Schuur and during my early days as consultant here," she said.

It was the long working hours that most bothered her. "As a registrar I was working flat-out at night. At Mowbray Maternity, for example, there was a Caesarean section every hour, so there was no chance of getting a rest. The senior doctors seemed to think that we were making up stories when we told them how hectic it was, so they weren't very sympathetic. They just didn't understand that the life of a doctor was now very different to when they were training. It was only when we undertook to keep a three-month log of our hours that they started to take our complaints seriously," she said.

"Did it make any difference?" I asked.

"No," she said wryly. "Groote Schuur is still stuck in the old way of doing things. But gradually the old guard is retiring, so those attitudes have to die out too."

The long hours continued when Vicky began working as a consultant. "I take my responsibilities very seriously, so I wouldn't leave a junior doctor to deal with a difficult case on their own or to anaesthetise a child. I often stayed to help them out but unfortunately that meant that I ended up working up to 60 hours per week. I started to feel resentful."

I could understand how such a gruelling schedule could have got to her. I noted that she didn't appear resentful any more. "How did you remedy that?" I asked.

She smiled broadly. "I took a year off to travel around the world," she said.

I was astounded and she laughed at my reaction. "How did you manage that?" I asked.

She was matter-of-fact about it. "I talked it over with my CEO, made sure that I had a competent replacement, and off I went. I had to take unpaid leave, of course, but I'd saved up so that wasn't a problem. The time away gave me an opportunity to think about what I wanted from my career, and I was clear when I got back that as much as I loved my work I didn't want to be married to it."

When Vicky returned to her job she came to an agreement with the doctor who had filled in for her during her year away. "We decided to split the post. So now I work three days a week and a total of 40 hours, including the after-hours calls."

"That's worked out well, then," I said.

"Yes, it's worked out very well. My doctor friends often ask what I do with the rest of my time because they can't imagine having so much free time. My non-medical friends, on the other hand, can't understand how I've *cut down* to 40 hours."

Vicky's innovative solution to the long working hours has attracted interest from other doctors. She frequently gets enquiries from doctors wanting to know how she's managed to do it. "I always give them the same advice. It boils down to good leadership. My CEO knows the ins and outs of HR policy, and more importantly he is willing to look at ways to work with the policy so that everyone wins."

Indeed Vicky seemed to be winning. I thought that the public health system was stuck, its legs knee-high in muck and mess. But listening to Vicky I felt a renewed sense of hope that change was possible. She had combined a long-term vision with a pragmatic and innovative approach to solving problems, measures that had resulted in significant changes in her environment. Above all, she was supported by a good leader.

I have to admit that, for the first time since leaving medicine, listening to Vicky made me think that I had made a mistake. It all seemed so doable. She had had a torrid time in the beginning, but she had looked ahead and not allowed herself to get too deeply embroiled in the prevailing circumstances. What if I'd stuck at it a little longer? Or at least worked to change the system from the outside as Francois had done?

As I walked away from more than two hours spent with Vicky thoughts churned in my head about the path that I'd veered from. I wondered if I should have tried harder to make things work. I too could have been part of a progressive medical family like the one that Vicky had created.

But as I took a final look at the hospital before driving out the gates and imagined myself arriving here or at a similar place every morning, the questions in my head were silenced by the resounding knowing in my heart: I just couldn't do it.

17 | Closing Up

It took me over a year to answer a nine-year-old question: why did I leave the medical profession? When I began this enquiry, in typical fashion I defaulted to the rational approach. I was presented with a question, and I aimed to answer it in the way I knew best – with diligent investigation, attention to detail and the careful piecing together of all the gathered evidence. I undertook to gather clues, both through interrogating my own story and by looking at the stories of others who had left.

As I began to speak to other doctors I fully expected that the answers would readily emerge, just as the bullet trail through the gangster's organs had told us that he had bled to death. That day at the mortuary I had watched as the technician had put the organs back in the man's torso. A part of me wanted to tell her to be more careful, to take care where she placed them, that the liver didn't belong on the left. But I quickly remembered that it didn't matter where she put them; their anatomically correct placement would do nothing to alter the outcome. I wanted to do the same here. I went looking for evidence, clues that I could piece together neatly to arrive at a coherent and definitive cause of death for my medical career. But the evidence hasn't quite come together in the way I had envisaged.

After all, this hasn't been a postmortem in the clinical sense. There are no scalpels, retractors, probes or beakers full of blood. It has been an enquiry in which I have asked myself difficult questions and out of which have come valuable insights. Although I was already having doubts about my medical career when I worked in the UK, I have also had to consider the role played by an important external factor: the dire state of the health care system in this country.

We've all seen the headlines before: the stories of under-resourced hospitals, patients dying on stretchers while waiting to be seen, babies dying because of faulty incubators, the assaults on doctors and nurses by patients in facilities where security is inadequate. There are many other stories from my interviews that I haven't included: junior doctors performing Caesarean sections while taking instructions from theatre sisters; community service doctors anaesthetising babies (a task that should only be delegated to experienced doctors) with disastrous consequences.

It irks me that practising medicine in South Africa's public hospitals is such a harrowing experience for many; that doctors work inhuman hours, in appalling conditions, and face numerous hazards associated with their work. It cannot continue to be the case that working as a doctor in the public health system is in itself an occupational hazard. What kind of service can be expected when doctors are overworked, stressed and under-appreciated?

Granted, the most harrowing experiences tend to be more prevalent during the early years of training, but what happens when these doctors move on to the private sector or become specialists? Where does the pain go? To what extent does it trickle down through the system and further contribute to the dysfunction? Ultimately it is the patients who suffer, the very people we are trying to serve.

I am also concerned that disparities in the provision of health care persist. It's not right that doctors work in under-resourced and poorly managed facilities. Who wins there? With the state of hospitals as they are, is it any wonder that we are facing such critical shortages of key personnel? Wouldn't you run to greener pastures too? It makes little sense to push to increase the number of students recruited into medical schools, to build more schools, or even to train more doctors in Cuba when they are going to be thrust into the same challenges when they qualify.

Vicky's case highlighted how good leadership can yield positive outcomes without putting unnecessary strain on the available resources. And as Ludwe pointed out – what is needed is competence and the will to do things differently. What a shame that someone like him, with both clinical and managerial skills, as well as the desire to make a difference, couldn't be put to use in the Eastern Cape's crumbling health care system. The much-vaunted National Health Insurance will do little to alleviate the crisis if these fundamentals are not adequately – and urgently – addressed.

Sometimes I can't help thinking that we permit ourselves to get away with the current state of our health care system because patients don't know any better. They are poor and uneducated, and they are desperate for the meagre resources that the public system provides. We get away with patients being attended by overworked, exhausted, disillusioned doctors; by inexperienced junior doctors who are poorly supervised. These poor patients have to wake up at dawn to make it to health facilities, and once there they have to wait to be seen. Faulty equipment and stock-outs of medicines leave them without the necessary tools to improve their health.

When I say *we* are getting away with it I mean all of us – doctors, medical schools, hospitals, health authorities, affluent patients who swear they will never use the public system. We also perpetuate the status quo by remaining silent, by asking that our stories be told on condition of anonymity, by not putting our hands up and asking for help. Poor, disenfranchised patients may not know any better, but they do deserve better.

Like so many other doctors who have left, medicine still occupies a special place in my heart. It saddens me that the stories contained in this book reflect so badly on what is really a noble and necessary profession. The medical profession places huge demands on doctors. This is not a purely South African phenomenon; it is common to medicine as a whole. Has the time not come for us to look at how we can preserve the best practices in the profession while getting rid of what no longer works? Does it really serve doctors to work long hours? Is there a rationale for this practice or is it merely something we do because that's how it's always been done? Now, more than ever, doctors need to have time for balance in their lives, because the need for their skills is so great.

Gone are the days when medicine was the sole preserve of men in white coats vying for a disease to be named after them. The rigid hierarchies and competitive environments that characterise our teaching institutions do little to cultivate a nurturing environment for students who will ultimately be expected to look after others. Learning by humiliation serves no one. Medicine is a service profession, and this imperative needs to underpin how medical students are selected and trained.

As doctors we need to take responsibility for our role in this mess. We don't do ourselves any favours by soldiering on. It needs to be okay for us to say that we are traumatised by our work. Also, it must be okay to say that the system of health care in this country contributes greatly to this trauma.

Who knows how differently my career would have turned out had I spoken up sooner, asked for help or even refused to work in an environment where I felt unsafe? What this postmortem has shown me is that I was too concerned about keeping up the pretence of coping and being in control when I would have been better served by allowing myself to be human. It is only now that I am putting my hand up to say that I was traumatised.

So did the public health system kill my medical career? I wish it was as straightforward as that. The path that my professional life took wasn't neat; various factors conspired to create the conditions that ultimately resulted in my decision to leave.

I was born into circumstances that could so easily have led to a life that is the story of so many black youths in our townships, where school dropouts, poverty and unemployment are commonplace. The foresight that my parents displayed in placing my education ahead of all other considerations ultimately gave me the break I needed, and I took full advantage of it. But even as I launched myself into my studies the unresolved pain and loss that I had experienced as a child lay just beneath the surface, and the pressures of medical school and later medical practice served to pick at the scab.

When I went out into the field I was faced with situations that I felt ill equipped to manage, and I became frustrated, angry and ultimately disillusioned. I no longer wanted to be around patients, to deal with their problems. Eventually I felt that the only way to save myself was to leave.

So it's all there – my brother Abbie, little Asive at Red Cross, the harrowing months at Jooste, the disillusionment that I felt so keenly in Khayelitsha.

There are other considerations too. How much did I really want it? To what extent was I seduced by what I perceived medicine to be? Perhaps if I'd felt that medicine was really where I wanted to be I would have tried harder to overcome the challenges I faced instead of allowing myself to succumb to them. All of these factors form important elements of my story.

I suspect that when people ask me why I stopped practising medicine I will continue to give them imprecise responses instead of the concise bottom-line-type answer I had hoped for. Only next time there won't be the accompanying discomfort that has previously characterised my responses. What this process has allowed me to do is to be okay with the fact that I let go of a dream.

The revelation came as quite a surprise. It crept up on me one morning as I was reviewing the doctors' stories in my head, looking for the pointers that would illuminate my own story. I noticed an unfamiliar feeling, a lightness I hadn't encountered before. I stopped to consider the source of the sensation. All I saw was the hint of a thread running through each of the stories, but it retreated as soon as I ventured to look closely. I put it out of my mind and carried on with my daily activities, though the sensation lingered in the background. I was rewarded at the end of the day when I realised what all the evidence had been pointing to all along: it wasn't just me.

Of course it wasn't just me. Why hadn't I seen that before? Was I too busy chastising myself to realise that I wasn't the only one who had struggled? I wasn't alone when, as an inexperienced graduate, I felt thrust into a role and entrusted with responsibilities that were out of proportion with what my training had provided. It wasn't just me who felt impotent in the face of overwhelming need. I wasn't the only one who had been frustrated by working in an environment where resources were limited and poorly managed. *Traumatic, unhealthy, crazy, overwhelming* . . . These words echoed through the many interviews with the doctors who had left.

The revelation was huge. For so long I had regarded my departure from medicine as a personal failing; I had buckled, failed to make the grade, been weak when resilience was really what was required. For someone who had based a large chunk of her identity on her ability to achieve, overcome challenges and persevere, the idea that I had succumbed had been difficult to bear. It came as a relief to realise that other bright, competent doctors had also struggled in their various ways.

It was the eminent physician and author, Dr Edward E Rosenbaum, who said: "There is no such thing as an infallible doctor." I interviewed dozens of former doctors during the course of writing this book and, for all the various reasons they chose to leave the medical profession, a common theme that ran through each of their stories was the realisation of their fallibility. In coming to terms with their own limitations and the constraints of the system under which they were working, they were able to walk away and begin again elsewhere.

When I met with these doctors our conversations often ran over the allotted time. Coffees would go cold as they shared their stories with me. I often got the impression that they were relieved by the opportunity to speak to someone who had been there and who understood what they had been through. Perhaps my sympathetic ear was a welcome change from the critical inner voice that is the constant companion of those of us who push ourselves to excel.

Ultimately it isn't necessary for my years in the medical profession to boil down to one convenient verdict. In much the same way as I had chased diagnoses as a student with little regard for what the patients were going through, I was chasing an answer here without paying attention to what was evident in the journey itself. To my mind what is far more important is what I have learned in undertaking it. After all, what difference will a definitive diagnosis make to the outcome? It was tough, it was sad, and then I left. That's all.

Epilogue

My daughter approaches, her brow furrowed to indicate she means business. I squeeze a smile from my lips and straighten up in my chair in preparation for the examination. This has become one of our favourite games; I play the sick patient, she the doctor. Her older sister, now seven years old, has long since lost interest in this game and she busies herself with her dolls on the floor.

The little one fiddles with the earpieces of my stethoscope – now a prop in their dress-up cupboard – before she expertly inserts them in her ears.

"Don't worry, Mommy. I promise it's not going to be sore," she assures me.

"Okay, Doctor," I say. I take a deep breath in when she places the diaphragm of the stethoscope on my chest. She nods thoughtfully as she moves the instrument around my chest, and I stifle a laugh when it wanders to my knee.

This is how I spend my afternoons, playing with my children and going about the chores that are my lot as a suburban mom. When the girls are at school in the morning I pursue my love of writing.

When I completed my work in provincial government after the FIFA World Cup in 2010 I found myself at yet another crossroads. My medical career had been over for six years, and I had tried my hand at a number of jobs and projects without feeling that I had found my fit.

One morning at home I was overcome by an irrational urge to write a novel. I say irrational because, although I have always been an avid reader, it had never occurred to me to write anything, and certainly not a novel. But the impulse was too strong to ignore, so I registered for a writing course to learn the craft. Thus began my life as a writer. Perhaps this is how all love affairs begin – with an irrational urge.

I couldn't have known then that by acting on a whim I was grasping the key that would finally enable me to open the door of my failed medical career, to take a thorough look inside, and then walk away, content that I had made the right decision.

"I'm done now, Mommy," my daughter says. She smiles broadly at me, pleased with herself. I return the smile.

Someday I will tell her about the time when I used to listen to people's chests. I will speak proudly of the little girl who dared to pursue her dream, about the hardships she experienced along the way, and I will make sure both my girls know that it's okay to stumble. For now I'm happy to play along with them.

"Mommy, you are all better now," she says as she walks away to join her sister.